Climate Action in the Art World

Hot Topics in the Art World

Published in association with Sotheby's Institute of Art

Series Editors

Jeffrey Boloten and Juliet Hacking, Sotheby's Institute of Art, London

This series of short, thought-provoking and sometimes controversial books debates key issues of current relevance to art-world professionals working in both the private and public sectors. The texts give wider visibility to some critical areas of professional art-world practice, considering what disruptors are challenging the status quo and how the art world is likely to be transformed over the next decades as a result.

International Series Advisory Board

Georgina Adam, journalist, author and art market Editor-at-Large of *The Art Newspaper*

Alia Al-Senussi, cultural strategist, patron, academic and lecturer

Touria El Glaoui, Founding Director of 1-54 Contemporary African Art Fair (London – New-York – Marrakech)

Jos Hackforth-Jones, former CEO and Director of Sotheby's Institute of Art, London

Louise Hamlin, Director of the Art Business Conference (London – New York – Shanghai)

Llucià Homs, Director of Talking Galleries, Barcelona

Zehra Jumabhoy, academic, critic and curator

Julie Lomax, CEO at a-n, The Artists Information Company, UK

Franklin Sirmans, Director of the Pérez Art Museum, Miami

Philip Tinari, Director and CEO of the UCCA Center for Contemporary Art, Beijing

Climate Action in the Art World

Towards a Greener Future

Annabel Keenan

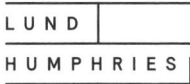

LUND
HUMPHRIES

Sotheby's INSTITUTE OF ART

First published in 2025 by Lund Humphries
in association with Sotheby's Institute of Art

Lund Humphries
Second Home Spitalfields
68–80 Hanbury Street
London E1 5JL
UK
info@lundhumphries.com
www.lundhumphries.com

ISBN (hardback): 978-1-84822-703-3
ISBN (eBook PDF): 978-1-84822-709-5
ISBN (eBook ePub): 978-1-84822-707-1

A Cataloguing-in-Publication record for this book is available from the
British Library

Copy edited by Michela Parkin
Designed by Crow Books
Set in Caslon Pro and Sofia Pro
Printed in Estonia

Lund Humphries' EU GPSR Authorised Representative is LOGOS
EUROPE, 9 rue Nicolas Poussin, 17000, LA ROCHELLE, France
Contact@logoseurope.eu

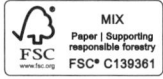

Contents

Foreword

When the wheels of the art-industry machinery ground to a standstill during the pandemic lockdowns, the environmental costs of much art-world activity and operations, particularly art fairs, international travel and the shipping of artworks, came into sharp focus. This period became the pivotal moment at which the industry finally confronted the enormity of the gap between its espousal of progressive views and its archaic practices as regards fossil fuels and wastage, and began the essential task of addressing the problems.

Writer, editor and curator Annabel Keenan has been consistently and intensively focused on the intersection of art and sustainability. In this compelling study, Keenan has consulted a wide range of art-industry players, including those working in galleries, art fairs, museums and, of course, artists themselves. Also closely studied and scrutinised in her investigations are key figures from supporting industries such as shipping, insurance and other related logistics partners within the global art ecosystem.

This pivotal book, combining new research with Keenan's art-industry analysis and expertise, provides an interdisciplinary and engaging perspective on the current problems, the issues that remain to be tackled urgently by the industry as a whole, and initiatives that provide sustainable alternatives to current practices. As Keenan highlights, there is a growing network of art-world professionals who are engaged in the research and development of new modalities and/or are committed to changing how they and their teams work. This book will hopefully add many more, much-needed hands for this campaign, ready and able to take the necessary next steps towards a sustainable, industry-wide paradigm shift.

Jeffrey Boloten and Juliet Hacking, January 2025

Acknowledgements

The literature on climate action in the art world is relatively nascent. The topic has certainly been a relevant issue for decades, but up until 2020, it wasn't a part of mainstream conversation in the industry. Before that time, many of the publications covering the intersection of art and climate were investigating how environmental disasters impact institutions, reporting on protests of oil sponsorships, or reviewing eco-themed artwork and exhibitions. Climate activists and groups promoting sustainable operations undoubtedly existed, some of which I discuss in this book, but climate action in the art world at the scale and enthusiasm in evidence today is new. We're only now seeing the impact the last few years of climate pledges and calls for action have had on the art industry. The topic is very much evolving and many of the sources used for this book are journalistic, written by me and a handful of others tracking the issues and progress.

I have many collaborators to thank who took the time to speak with me and share their insight for this book, including Haley Mellin, Laura Lupton, Heath Lowndes, Cliodhna Murphy, Larissa Harris, Andrea Andersson, Alex Klein, James Merle Thomas and Maureen Bray. There are also many people and groups whose work I've followed for years and who have generously shared their knowledge and expertise in climate action not just with me, but with the general public. Among the groups crucial for me to thank for shaping my understanding of climate action in the art world are Artists Commit, Galleries Commit, Gallery Climate Coalition, Ki Culture and Art Switch.

As a writer, especially a freelance one, I can only write what someone is willing to publish. I am grateful for my current and former editors at *The Art Newspaper*, Ben Sutton, Elena Goukassian and Helen Stoilas, who encourage my focus on climate action and have given me the platform to showcase the work being done in the industry.

Introduction

Out of the 'hot topics' in the art world that this series takes as its subject, climate action is quite literally the hottest. In 2023 the world experienced the hottest summer on record. In September of that year, the United Nations Secretary-General António Guterres issued a statement declaring that climate breakdown has begun.[1] Simply put, with climate breakdown we have reached the point where the impact of human activities is causing changes that are extremely harmful, result in the loss of biodiversity and are potentially irreversible. In 2024 the world experienced yet another blistering summer, surpassing 2023 as the record hottest. Indeed, for several long weeks while writing this book, I and millions of other people across the United States faced oppressive temperatures as heatwaves stifled much of the country. The heat is only one of many climate issues we and the rest of the world are facing. In August 2024 one of the largest wildfires in California's history ravaged the state. In September 2024 Storm Boris brought record-breaking rain and devastating floods to Central Europe, displacing thousands and killing at least 26 people. These weather events are bringing issues of the climate crisis to the fore: the vulnerability of underserved communities; the disproportionate access to clean water and clean air; the increasing intensity, frequency and devastating impact of weather events; the irrefutable urgency of the need to change our behaviours and mitigate the damage we've done; and the reality of how unprepared we truly are.

This introduction will outline the things I can and can't cover in a single book with as broad a subject as the art world and as complex a lens as climate action. My goal is to simplify and summarise complicated and nuanced topics to speak to a broad audience. While I discuss technical and scientific terms, I have tried to do so in a way that is accessible. A reader with climate expertise may find some details glossed over, but I've done my best to note where more information is available. This book is not encyclopaedic. Many books can, and should, be written about climate action in the art world (and the arts more broadly, as significant work is being done in theatre and music, for example). I hope my work can contribute to a larger conversation and that many other voices join.

There is a vast, global network working to make the art world sustainable. This network and its activities evolve alongside the issues as we adapt as an industry and respond to changes in policy and perspective (within the sector and governmentally), as well as to collective and individual needs. Between finishing this book and when it is published, I expect new developments will have occurred. Such changes are not only inevitable, but also necessary. We must constantly evaluate the needs of every aspect of the industry and adapt accordingly.

In this book, I focus in particular on New York, Los Angeles and London, because these are the regions that I, as a New York-based writer, cover most often. Moreover, ideas and approaches to sustainability vary worldwide and can depend on local regulations and attitudes towards the topic. In China, for example, museums are primarily state-owned and are subject to different operational principles than, say, a privately owned museum in New York. That's not to say work isn't being done where governments wield greater power over cultural institutions, but the definition of sustainability can differ and focus, for example, on financial sustainability. My relatively local approach reflects the nascent state of widespread conversations around climate action in the art world and the need to strengthen global engagement as an entire industry. I have included global examples when possible. While geographically limited, the topics I cover are intentionally ambitious and include the commercial sector, as well as the non-profit side. I cover big museums, small institutions, art fairs, galleries and grant-giving organisations. I touch on the supporting industries, such as shipping. And, of course, I write about artists and art. In taking this ambitious approach, I hope to illustrate that climate action relates to everyone at every level and in every environment.

The terms climate action and sustainability are broad and subjective. Sustainability can be a contradictory word, as one definition means the sustaining or maintaining of a certain state. In relation to the environment, sustainability refers to the state of being that avoids permanently damaging or depleting natural resources, a state that often requires going against the status quo. Environmental sustainability, therefore, cannot be achieved through sustaining existing practices unless every level of those practices ensures an equitable, green future. Climate action is more expansive. Climate action includes climate justice, and issues of climate justice overlap with social justice and diversity, equity and inclusion. The impetus for some climate actions might be the desire to improve a practice, while for others it might be fighting for survival in the face of environmental racism, a term that refers to any policy or system that leads to the disproportionate exposure of marginalised communities to environmental issues, such as poor air or polluted water. Climate action isn't just about climate change. Some of the most powerful artworks I've seen speak to issues of air quality and land rights – topics that overlap with sustainability and climate action, but might not fall squarely in what one thinks of as climate change. Moreover, what I call climate action may simply be the way of life for people who live closer to the land. Many sustainable practices are based on Indigenous knowledge. Their relationship with the land is one of equality, kinship, cultivation and stewardship, a relationship that can offer solutions to mitigate the extractive practices causing problems with the environment today.

The art world can amplify climate issues and serve as a tool for education and activism. The bulk of this book focuses on climate action since 2020, but groups and initiatives existed before this. In the United Kingdom, the non-profit Julie's Bicycle has been leveraging cultural and environmental expertise to promote climate action since 2007. Julie's Bicycle works with groups across cultural industries, including visual arts and music, and has partnered with over 2000 organisations worldwide. The non-profit offers support in a number of ways, such as providing coaching and practical tools for carbon-footprint calculations.

In 2019 another group emerged that marked the beginning of climate awareness in the art world for many individuals and institutions: Culture Declares Emergency. While founded in the UK, the group has formed several international hubs, and its declaration has been adopted by many institutions to guide their own climate pledges. The declaration begins: 'We declare that the Earth's life-supporting systems are in collapse, threatening biodiversity and human societies everywhere',[2] and continues with an acknowledgement of the power structures that silence marginalised voices and further ecocide, as well as a call for arts and culture professionals to take action.

In the years between these two moments, several other climate initiatives emerged, some of which are discussed in this book, but my focus is on 2020 onwards. When COVID-19 forced nations into lockdown and shuttered non-essential businesses, the art industry, like so many others, found itself in a moment of self-reflection. As lockdowns prevented us from leaving our homes to go to the galleries, museums, studios and institutions we normally frequent, artists and art workers saw a shift in the norm. Exhibitions were postponed, loans were cancelled, art fairs went digital and, for the first time perhaps in art history, the operations of the art world were put under a magnifying glass. Industry standards and best practices across the board came under scrutiny, issues amplified by a global reckoning with the rapidly deteriorating climate, as well as the spread of the Black Lives Matter movement. Individuals in all industries began to reflect on their role as global citizens while living remarkably interior lives. At the same time, taking accountability and standing up for what is right became increasingly common. Against the backdrop of this intense period of insecurity, change and accountability, emerged a movement in the art world that many had been quietly working to support, or agreed with but didn't have the tools or language to name: climate action.

In the years since 2020, sustainability groups have emerged worldwide, from the artist-led Artists Commit to the industry-centred Gallery Climate Coalition, think-tanks like Ki Culture, and climate-focused grants from organisations like Teiger Foundation. In Chapter 1, I discuss how the art world has begun to identify wasteful practices, calculate the industry's climate impact and take steps to find best practices. In addressing the sector's issues, superfluous practices have been increasingly scrutinised, such as excessively flying artwork and people across the world to attend private viewings and art fairs. In this chapter, I also highlight the need to work with the art world's supporting industries like shippers and insurance companies to find holistic, long-term solutions.

As institutions and individuals address the industry's climate impact, artists have responded in kind. Artists are the lifeblood of the art world. In Chapter 2, I highlight some of the artists who have made the environment and climate change their subject, creating work that centres regeneration, illuminates the negative repercussions of climate change and encourages viewers to think beyond the human-centric. This chapter also explores how studio practices have been improved, with groups like Artists Commit sharing tips on sustainable materials and offering mentorship on how to advocate for climate-conscious exhibitions. And, regardless of whether the reader agrees with it or not, art in general has become a conduit for conversations on climate change as groups like Just Stop Oil have made the museum a space for activism and protest, for better or worse. These protests are part of climate action in the art world.

In Chapter 3, I highlight case studies of climate action by institutions, including galleries and museums, underscoring the important work of grant-giving organisations, climate specialists and groups supporting green initiatives. There are certain climate actions that have become more common, such as carbon-footprint calculations and waste-reduction plans. Many efforts are in alignment with the Paris Agreement on climate change and aim to reduce greenhouse gas emissions across the entire industry by 50 per cent by 2030 and achieve net zero by 2050. And finally, Chapter 4 considers the future of climate action in the art world and some of the small and large ways the industry still needs to improve. I hope this final chapter serves not as the end of the conversation but the beginning of another, as changes continue to be made and voices continue to join the ongoing fight against climate change.

It almost seems unnecessary to explain my 'why' for this book. I can't step outside on a summer day without thinking of 'why'. The climate is breaking down. The world is burning, flooding and crumbling. Planet-wide behavioural change is necessary to fix the damage we've done. My 'why' for the art world is more specific, and one I'm reminded of constantly. The fact is that climate action is not currently being taken seriously across the entire industry. I often feel like my work exists in a bubble, and to some degree it does. When I explain my speciality, I'm often met with scepticism and surprise that such a topic even relates to the art world. Just recently, upon meeting someone for the first time, I was asked if climate action is 'wallpaper' so we can feel good about doing bad. Climate action is still a young, nebulous part of the industry and we are only now seeing a concerted push for system-wide change. There is much work to be done, and I hope this book inspires interest and offers a path towards action.

1

Identifying the Issues

To fix any problem, you must first admit that it exists. Unfortunately, despite scientific evidence and first-hand experiences with the effects of climate change, there are still people who deny its existence. Then there are people who accept that climate change is a fact, but deny our personal and collective responsibilities in addressing and mitigating the problem. Knowledge, it seems, does not equate to action. In the fight against climate change, we are as responsible in our own homes as we are in our communities. The art world is no exception.

There are currently no extensive studies of the entire art sector's impact on the environment, but internal analyses, annual estimates,[1] smaller surveys and groupings of reports (see Chapters 2 and 3) are becoming more common to set baselines and benchmarks. Regardless of this lack of comprehensive analysis, there is a general consensus based on estimates that the impact of the art industry is small compared to something like fashion. However, we cannot compare apples to oranges. The perception of our impact relative to other industries shouldn't be an arbiter of whether or not to act. We must act, and we can always work towards better practices. There are areas for improvement within the art industry, including some glaring norms whose waste far outweighs their utility. This chapter explores some of the issues that climate-action groups and specialists have identified over the years as needing improvement within the art world, as well as the roadblocks the industry faces in implementing them.

Certain overlapping goals continue to come to the fore that define how the art world even begins to understand and mitigate its impact on the environment. These goals generally centre on reducing waste, aligning efforts, sharing resources and working to maintain the standards set by the Paris Agreement (also called the Paris Accord) at the UN Climate Change Conference (COP 21) in 2015. This legally binding treaty sets long-term goals, in particular to 'substantially reduce global greenhouse gas emissions to hold global temperature increase to well below 2°C above pre-industrial levels and pursue efforts to limit it to 1.5°C above pre-industrial levels, recognizing that this would significantly reduce the risks and impacts of climate change'.[2] This goal is referenced in many of the mission statements and climate-action plans of the individuals and institutions discussed in this book, as is the term 'net zero'. The Paris Agreement offers a path towards net zero, which needs to be reached by 2050 to keep within the requirements of the agreement.[3] As the UN states: 'Put simply, net zero means cutting carbon emissions to a small amount of residual emissions that can be absorbed and durably stored by nature and other carbon dioxide removal measures, leaving zero in the atmosphere'.[4] The UN also sets 2030 as a benchmark to stay in line with the Paris Accord, stating, 'To limit global warming to 1.5°C, greenhouse gas emissions must peak before 2025 at the latest and decline 43% by 2030'.[5] Globally, strong evidence indicates we are far off track to achieving the standards of the Paris Accord and nowhere near the target of 2030.

Carbon Footprints

The Paris Accord is a clear goal for the art world, but there is no singular roadmap to reaching it. It does, thankfully, introduce quantitative standards in the form of carbon emissions. This can certainly present challenges, as it requires specialised knowledge to calculate, analyse and reduce carbon emissions, which is where climate groups and consultants provide specialised tools and expertise and have made the biggest impact in catalysing system-wide change.

As mentioned in the Introduction, Julie's Bicycle, which launched in the UK in 2007, has assisted over 2000 art and culture organisations worldwide in improving their operations, often through the use of their carbon-footprint calculator. Simply explained, the Greenhouse Gas Protocol (GHG) sets standards for tracking carbon footprints worldwide and divides emissions into three scopes: 'Scope 1 emissions are direct emissions from owned or controlled sources; Scope 2 emissions are indirect emissions from the generation of purchased energy; Scope 3 emissions are all indirect emissions (not included in scope 2) that occur in the value chain of the reporting company, including both upstream and downstream emissions'.[6] Scopes 1 and 2 generally refer to the actions that an organisation or individual can control.[7] Carbon-footprint calculations commonly take into consideration scopes 1 and 2 of carbon emissions, but exclude or estimate scope 3.

In addition to working with Julie's Bicycle, several organisations and individuals in the art world have used the carbon calculator created by the global charity Gallery Climate Coalition (GCC). The charity, which was founded in 2020 by a group of dealers, writers, artists and industry leaders in London who came together to share their concerns for the pitfalls of sustainability in the art industry and their frustration with the lack of information and guidelines available, has been involved with countless forms of climate action. In addition to the carbon calculator, GCC's website contains a wealth of information on sustainable practice, and the work it has undertaken to support the industry is cited many times in this book. GCC now has over 1500 members (artists, non-profits, institutions, suppliers, galleries) from more than 50 countries and has branches in Berlin, Italy, Los Angeles, New York and Taiwan, though in September 2024 the group announced the closure of all chapters outside the UK, citing a lack of funding to support them and an overall need to reevaluate the best path forward for a global network (see Chapter 4).[8]

Virtually every aspect of the art world has a carbon footprint. Conducting carbon reports is a useful tool to identify areas where individuals and institutions can make changes to reduce their emissions, whether that's through consolidating shipping, switching to renewable energy sources or simply changing the type of lightbulb used to illuminate an artwork. Examples of such steps are explored throughout this book. Carbon calculations of individual actions like shipments or entire exhibitions and annual operations are becoming more commonplace in the industry. The more reporting we have, the better we can understand how to improve on individual and collective levels.

Waste

Reducing carbon emissions offers a calculable path towards a greener industry, but other issues are more difficult to track. Like the rest of the planet, one of the challenges facing the art industry is waste. Waste goes hand in hand with carbon emissions as an important target to minimise. The term waste is nuanced, and can be taken to mean a superfluous practice, as well as unusable surplus materials. Within the art world, waste is a problem amplified by the individualised, temporary nature of many aspects of the industry. For example, exhibitions often require institutions to redesign spaces, such as with custom-built walls and fresh paint. While many institutions make efforts to store materials for reuse, this is often limited to smaller items like plinths and crates, not purpose-built walls. Much of what is left over, unusable or unable to be stored ends up in landfill. In the case of museums, exhibition redesigns might occur a few times per year, allowing for time to plan for waste management, but in the commercial sector galleries are accustomed to changing shows more frequently, sometimes monthly. For institutions working at a faster pace, it's harder to implement waste-management plans. It's not uncommon to walk down the streets of Chelsea in New York and see empty art-packing crates tossed on the sidewalk. However, while a longer exhibition can allow for better planning, that doesn't mean that efforts to minimise waste are the norm, and the onus of developing and implementing such plans often falls on individuals who take on the task on top of their busy workloads.

On a small scale, though, efforts are being made to create systems of reducing waste. In 2019 the online Circular Arts Network (CAN) launched in Scotland, enabling users in the UK to advertise items (anything from packing material to furniture) and services (transportation, fabrication etc.), offering them for free or at low prices. In 2020 Jae Cho, a New York-based climate activist and director of Spencer Brownstone Gallery, began a similar peer-to-peer resource-sharing website where users anywhere in the world can advertise materials like crates, lighting, packing materials and audio-visual equipment, also for free or for sale. Called Barder, the platform officially launched in 2022 after over a year in a beta phase when Cho and co-founder Laura Lupton worked mainly with institutions in New York and Los Angeles to build the user-base. Since then, Barder has grown to encompass international users, including from London and Berlin.

Energy

At times, industry-wide standards can be the culprits responsible for waste and high carbon emissions. Across the board, unnecessarily strict climate-control requirements for the display of artworks at (mainly Western) institutions result in increased energy consumption due to the power needed to operate the monitors and systems for climate regulation. According to Caitlin Southwick, a former conservator for the Vatican Museums in Rome and founder of Ki Culture (an Amsterdam-based non-profit that offers sustainability training and resources for cultural heritage organisations and workers), these requirements, which are based on old conservation standards set after World War II by institutions evaluating collections in cold, wet cities, are now implemented in completely different environments and often exceed the needs of individual artworks and collections.[9] Efforts are underway to reconsider these strict standards (see Chapter 3). For example, in the autumn of 2022, the Guggenheim Bilbao changed its climate-control standards to allow for a wider range of temperature and humidity in some galleries, a decision that reduced its energy bill by 20,000 euros per month.[10]

Climate-control standards also have repercussions for loans of artwork between institutions, as they require borrowers to follow regulations that might exceed their own standards and increase energy consumption. Not all institutions can satisfy loan requirements, leading to inequity and limiting access for many areas and cultures, in particular the Global South. When the Guggenheim Bilbao implemented its more flexible temperature and humidity standards, it did so with an exhibition of works entirely from its collection and was therefore able to loosen the requirements. For future exhibitions, the museum is requiring lenders to adhere to its standards as opposed to the other way around, which they've reported has generally not been an issue.[11] The Guggenheim's insistence on change is a significant example of how institutions can use their power to advocate for a greener industry. Such activism is necessary at all levels, but those with international reach and regard wield greater potential for broader, immediate change.

This, however, requires institutions to be open to shaking up the status quo. In general, across all industries in the modern, capitalist society in which we live, sustaining the system is viewed as stability. Within the art world, Caitlin Southwick calls this an obsession with professionalism. 'Professionalism is linked to inertia', she argues. 'The climate conversation requires questions, it requires challenging current practices, and it may be seen as a disturbance.'[12] However, if the status quo is not working towards a green future, it cannot be considered sustainable. Maria Balshaw, Director of Tate, put it succinctly: 'Through our ability to use energy, technology and science to get to near-perfect conservation, we become exceptionally carbon consumptive. We need to talk more openly about making pragmatic choices that would protect the collections in our care but not so "perfectly", prioritizing the planetary impact and the benefit to people from learning about and enjoying the art.'[13] Indeed, as climate change worsens, all institutions must be open to reevaluating their operations. Balshaw's call for change and the

Guggenheim Bilbao's resistance of wasteful standards are important models for green leaders in the industry.

Shipping

Transportation of artwork and people is an area undeniably ripe for improvement. Artwork is typically shipped via air, road or rail, and less frequently via sea. Each method has different requirements and comes with its own carbon footprint. In a GCC case study of the transportation of Gary Hume artworks from London to Matthew Marks Gallery in New York, shipping via sea had a carbon footprint 96 per cent lower than what it would have been if air freight had been used.[14] It should be noted, however, that sea freight is not always the best option. For example, if the artwork is not located near a major port, it may take additional transfers and energy expenditure for it to reach that port. What might be sustainable in one circumstance may not be so in another, making it difficult to make blanket statements for best practices. Rather, the most sustainable option will have to be determined case by case.

The strict climate-control standards of loans of artworks from one organisation to another also apply to the shipping environments of these loans and can make certain options unviable. Again, this is case by case depending on the requirements of a loan (some might not allow for sea freight, for example). In considering the carbon footprint of a shipment, it should also be noted that some loans require couriers to accompany the work, which is often the case for high-value artworks. The COVID-19 pandemic brought worldwide travel bans, which saw the use of virtual couriers, digital tools that can track the artwork's location in transit and provide condition information. Some, like ParceLive, have light sensors that track when a crate is opened and can sense the temperature and movement of the piece, recording, for example, if the package is tilted. These courier systems can also provide messaging platforms for streamlined communication, such as Articheck, which also allows users to store information like condition reports. Virtual couriers reduce carbon emissions by removing the need for staff members to travel with the work. In 2020 Tate Modern used virtual couriers to deinstall and transport high-value loans from its *Andy Warhol* exhibition to Museum Ludwig, Cologne. 'It was nerve-wracking to begin with', Tate Director Maria Balshaw writes. 'But, in fact, this temporary arrangement allowed us to gain significant experience in lending and borrowing securely, without the safety blanket of a physical courier.'[15] Tate now operates with a virtual-first courier policy and has signed a Memorandum of Understanding with the Museum of Modern Art, New York to use virtual couriers for loans between the institutions. Collaboration and change, it seems, are possible.

There is no doubt that shipping is a necessary practice in the art industry, but it can easily get out of hand, particularly on the commercial side. It's a poorly kept secret that blue-chip galleries are accustomed to shipping works of art across countries for private viewings by individual collectors or purchasers. Again, a courier might be used. If a work is valuable enough, or if the collector is deemed important enough, this also includes international travel for both the artwork and the accompanying courier. These shipping practices partly stem from the competition and lack of transparency inherent in the commercial art sector. Say, for example, that I'm hoping to sell a US$20 million painting to a private collector in a remote town in France, so I decide to fly the work from Los Angeles to France for a viewing. I might not want to put it on a consolidated shipment with work from another gallery, as this might risk revealing the identity of the potential buyer, and a competing gallery could fly its top salesperson to the same remote town armed with PDFs of their own coveted inventory and ruin my sale. Maybe the work I'm offering was only purchased last year, or maybe it's a painting so wet it has barely left the artist's studio, and I could risk blacklisting the seller for 'flipping', a practice generally frowned upon in which a collector resells a work shortly after acquiring it for a profit, oftentimes a significant profit. Maybe I don't even have the consignment, and I'm taking a bold move out of desperation to show the seller that I have a potential buyer, therefore beating out another dealer vying for the consignment. To secure the deal, I'll also fly to France, adding my own carbon footprint to that of the flight and truck transfers it takes to transport the work. I wish these were exaggerations, but anyone who has caught a glimpse behind the blue-chip curtain has heard of or facilitated similar scenarios. In an industry with few regulations, serious lack of transparency and high financial stakes, paranoia and competition abound.

The same goes for auction houses that tour high-value works or entire sales across their global network to give clients worldwide a chance to sample their goods in person. These international displays can be a branding tool for the auction house to attract new buyers and sellers, as well as a means to assure their consignors that every effort was undertaken to market the works for sale. The record-shattering US\$450.3 million sale of Leonardo da Vinci's *Salvator Mundi* (*c*.1500) at Christie's, New York in 2017 followed a viewing tour that included stops in Hong Kong, London, San Francisco and New York. Regardless of the remarkable monetary, historic and cultural value of the work, the admissibility of the carbon footprint of its grand tour is questionable. An argument could be made about giving a global audience the opportunity to view a work that remained largely unseen for centuries. Moreover, one could contend that by bringing the work to collectors in their own cities and countries, the auction house avoided the carbon footprint of the flights viewers would have taken to visit the piece in another location. The case of *Salvator Mundi* serves as a public example of what happens in the art world behind closed doors. As private institutions, galleries and some auction houses have little more than their own ethical standards holding them accountable. (I will note that in 2021 Christie's became the first major auction house to establish a sustainability strategy to reduce emissions by 50 per cent and neutralise its carbon impact by 2030, and has hosted charitable auctions to raise funds for climate action, discussed in Chapter 3.)[16]

For museums and non-profits, shipping practices are relatively less frivolous, as these spending-conscious organisations tend to have fewer resources to draw on and therefore have to plan more carefully to reduce the number of flights needed to stage a show. Museums also traditionally have their exhibition schedules planned further in advance than commercial galleries, which creates opportunities to choose slower, less energy-consuming options like sea and rail (if indeed these are the best options for the particular scenario). Moreover, some artists and institutions are now advocating for exhibitions that source from local lenders, thus reducing shipping (see Chapter 2). The COVID-19 lockdowns brought broader application and acceptance of the digital realm, as well as improved tools to experience art virtually, increasing the use of online exhibitions and sales. Additionally, as conversations on sustainability in the art world have become more common in recent years, members of the public and the press are becoming more vocal in their calls for transparency and waste reduction. We now live in a society accustomed to calling out those in the wrong and – while there is risk inherent in policing (and cancelling) one another – we are in the midst of an overall shift towards greater accountability.

Supporting Industries

As calls for green practices become more common, the industries that support the art world are evolving in response. Shipping companies, for example, are increasingly offering more sustainable options. In 2023 the GCC conducted a survey in which twelve major shipping companies participated. According to the survey results, nearly all of the companies had published sustainability statements online and were taking various steps to implement sustainable practices. For example, all twelve companies offer alternatives to air freight. Eleven were working to implement best practices for packaging to reduce waste (the twelfth, Arta, was in the process of taking this step as of 2023). Some companies include data for carbon-emissions reporting on their invoices to help their clients understand the impact of their shipments and make climate-conscious decisions. The full survey is available online.[17]

Among the shipping companies leading the sustainable charge is Gander & White, which has locations across Europe and the US and is a member of GCC, including among its initiatives: reusing or recycling crates, offering sea freight, reducing its carbon emissions by 2.5 per cent annually and committing to net zero by the end of 2024. Along with Haas & Company, Dietl and Helutrans, Gander & White is also a partner and official supplier of ROKBOX LOOP, a reusable crate rental programme. ROKBOX also offers their reusable, recyclable crates for purchase as opposed to renting them.

The topic of crates brings us to another issue with sustainability: packing materials. Generally, packing materials used to transport and store art, like foam and bubble wrap, are synthetic and created with fossil fuels and can take generations to biodegrade, if at all. Moreover, materials like plastic wrap and bubble wrap are easily ripped during unpacking, so it can be difficult to reuse them. Though many of these materials are recyclable, they are not typically curbside recyclable, meaning they are not able to be picked up by your local collector and instead need to be brought to a recycling centre or other specialised facility. This is not always obvious (and can even be misleading), and what can and cannot be recycled varies regionally. These materials are also difficult to sort and some, like plastic wrap and gloves, are known to clog machines, so some recycling facilities don't take them. Ultimately, non-curbside recyclable materials often end up incinerated or in landfills.[18]

While some fossil fuel-derived traditional packing materials are resilient and therefore can be reused many times, they are subject to the same issues that apply to reusing items like crates and plinths – they have to be stored and many works require custom-made packaging. Moreover, for high-value artworks, insurance companies might require new crates and packing materials. Indeed, in general, insurance is an area where there is room for improvement. Historically, fine-art insurers have viewed sea freight as a riskier option due to a variety of factors (climate on board the ship, longer duration of travel etc.). Insurers might exclude sea freight coverage if air freight is possible, or they may impose higher premiums and stricter conditions for sea freight. Progress has been made to include insurance companies in the broader conversation on climate action in the art world, and galleries like Hauser & Wirth and groups like GCC have noted fruitful conversations with insurers that have expanded coverage of greener shipping options.[19] The more we ask for sustainable options, the more the supporting industries will provide them.

Art Fairs

All of this brings us to the elephant in the room: art fairs. As temporary ventures, art fairs face several challenges in terms of sustainability, which vary based on the event. Untitled Art in Miami, for example, takes place directly on the beach in a temporary tent. For sustainability and cost purposes, the fair reuses the same tent each year, but constructs new auxiliary spaces like VIP lounges. Untitled Art works with Miami's Department of Environmental Protection to ensure the fair leaves 'zero-impact' on the fragile, eroding sands of Miami Beach, meaning that once the fair is over, the beach must be left the same way it was found.[20] Fairs held inside existing buildings have their own set of challenges, including building temporary walls, installing energy-consuming lighting and dealing with waste from exhibitors and attendees. Some fairs are in buildings with specific sustainability requirements that they must adhere to, such as Art Basel Miami Beach in the Miami Beach Convention Center, which holds the level of Silver on the Leadership in Energy and Environmental Design (LEED) rating system. The global programme assesses building energy efficiency, as well as environmental, governance and social benefits on a four-tiered scale, with Silver as the third-highest ranking.

As an art-fair exhibitor, it can be difficult to maintain climate-conscious standards. According to GCC, art fair-related activities are estimated to account for a third of the annual carbon emissions for a commercial gallery.[21] Waste reduction is also difficult at fairs, as some of the packing materials needed to ship art may not be able to be stored during the fair for reuse after. Making sustainable decisions on shipping in general can be challenging. For some dealers, fairs are an opportunity to display an artist's newest pieces, which can mean the artist is still working on them close to opening day. This would make more climate-conscious options like road, ocean or rail freight impossible, as they are slower and require longer lead times. In general, because these methods of transport demand a more flexible timeline to account for delays (in particular ocean freight's susceptibility to potential weather and customs setbacks), they are often challenging for exhibitors to use for art fairs, which require more precise shipping deadlines. This doesn't mean it's impossible to implement best practices, but there are significant roadblocks. Shipping companies are working to support exhibitors in this respect, with most of the major companies that participated in GCC's 2023 shipper survey reporting that they currently publish or are in the process of promoting deadlines for sea and road shipments for major fairs and events.[22]

Amplifying these issues is the highly competitive nature of art fairs. The paranoia around the hypothetical US$20 million painting flying to France is ten-fold with a fair, where the high costs of participation (booth fees, shipping, flights, accommodations and dinners) add additional pressure to make sales. Galleries don't want to share what they're bringing with each other in advance, and some of the works shipped to fairs are intended for private viewing rooms, so dealers might book private shuttles instead of joining a consolidated shipment. Moreover, the sense of urgency latent in the industry is equally heightened, with last-minute decisions to add high-value consignments or unexpected works fresh from a studio requiring last-minute flights.

Planning for the return trip is particularly tricky, as exhibitors don't know the final destination of the works until they are sold, if at all. When the event ends, booths are quickly deinstalled so that fair organisers can take down temporary walls and clear out the spaces they themselves are only renting. The post-fair activities are, therefore, expedited. Some artworks may be pre-sold and their shipments determined in advance, but in general planning has to be flexible. There are nuances with each fair and each exhibitor. Some galleries might have locations near the fair or have the resources to rent space in a nearby storage facility, giving extra time after the fair to receive payments from collectors and coordinate shipping. Other galleries might not have the resources for these kinds of facilities and might have to quickly arrange for works to travel to their buyer on the hoof. This transfer of goods and ownership can be a grey area for sustainability. And, of course, those works that are not sold must travel somewhere after the fair, whether that's back to the gallery, the artist's studio or storage.

On top of this, art fairs require many people to fly across the country and the world to staff the booths. Art Basel's 2024 edition in Switzerland featured 285 galleries from over 40 countries and territories. It's safe to assume that multiple staff from each gallery travelled to Basel, most of whom likely took international flights. The same event saw 91,000 visitors in attendance.[23] While this number hopefully comprises local audiences, it is undeniable numerous flights were taken. For its part, Art Basel is attempting to account for these factors. The fair encourages low-carbon travel and asks shippers to specify the distances and means of transport and the weight of artworks in order to better understand the impact of its partners and collaborators.[24]

Despite best efforts to encourage climate-conscious, low-carbon travel, art fairs are not in control of the behaviour of exhibitors and attendees, some of whom will undoubtedly be wealthy individuals accustomed to flying privately. A 2023 study by the UK charity Possible indicates that the use of private jets increased significantly after the pandemic with one flight in every ten departing from UK airports being a private jet flight.[25] It's well documented that private jets have a significant carbon footprint, ten times more than a normal flight per person, according to Greenpeace.[26] As *The Art Newspaper*'s Louisa Buck noted, the use of private planes in the art world is widely known, as the industry's close connections with the world's wealthiest people gives ample access to private jets, and one mega-gallery owner has admitted to using his plane to fly between the gallery's 19 locations worldwide. Buck also pointed to the presence of private jet companies at art fairs, including official partnerships between NetJets and Art Basel, as well as VistaJet and Frieze, though the latter relationship has ended.[27] While it's unlikely galleries will police the activities of their collectors and refuse to sell to private flyers, they can at least ban the use of private planes for company activities, and fairs can ask the same of their partners. However, I find it hard to believe anyone would be willing to tell their mega-dealer boss to fly commercial.

Now What? How to Tackle the Issues

There are many roadblocks, from the existential to the logistical, for individuals and institutions to begin to address sustainability and take actionable steps. Perhaps the most difficult part of taking action is understanding where to start. We are at the inception of climate action as a concerted movement in the art world, so there is no one clear starting point. Indeed, it may not be possible to have just one. No two operations or issues are identical, and there are no master plans or easy solutions. The groups and collectives discussed throughout this book are great places to start and can help in countless ways, whether it's by providing a community to crowdsource information or helping to establish tailored plans through consulting and coaching. Feeling unprepared or unsure of what climate action and sustainability will look like shouldn't preclude someone from taking action. The best place to start is anywhere.

Compounding the question of where to start is understanding who is responsible for doing the work. Individuals, such as artists, can make these decisions on their own, but in institutions things get murky. Employees may feel a moral obligation to encourage climate action in all aspects of their lives, including professionally, but they also must maintain their jobs to survive and are not always in the position to advocate for change. Employers can feel equally driven to improve the operations of their companies (assuming they have the agency to do so), but putting the onus on their employees can strain already exhausted resources. Some institutions are hiring in-house sustainability positions and external consultants, which requires funding. Others are forming 'green teams' of volunteers, but these are not always sustainable to maintain.

Another common hurdle is the apprehension around opening one's organisation up to scrutiny. There are multiple layers to this, one being that if we reframe scrutiny as accountability, then holding this kind of magnifying glass to our own actions is a positive thing. However, while we should all hold ourselves and each other accountable in the climate crisis, it is not one person's or institution's responsibility to solve every problem. A further layer is that, frankly, the fear of climate breakdown should outweigh the fear of being scrutinised as a less-than-perfect climate declarant. Eventually, we will not have the luxury of this fear.

Funding

Beyond the existential, the art industry faces a concrete issue of funding, a problem heightened during the pandemic. According to a July 2020 survey from the American Alliance of Museums, one in three museums in the US was at risk of closing due to the economic impact of COVID-19.[28] In 2024 in New York, we saw the closure of the Center for Italian Modern Art, as well as the downsizing of the Rubin Museum of Art to shift to a lending institution. Regardless of how financially successful or well funded an organisation is, allocating resources can be a challenging, long process. Commercial or privately funded ventures are relatively more flexible in terms of earmarking resources for specific causes, but institutions beholden to boards and public stakeholders, or burdened by years of deficit, often face complex, arduous bureaucratic processes to decide how resources are spent.

It can be difficult to allocate funds to climate action when institutions are struggling to survive and when other issues exist, such as neglected or failing infrastructures. Oftentimes, institutions are forced to respond to environmental disasters when they occur instead of using funds for climate resilience. Climate change is an urgent issue. It needs urgent funding that cannot be bogged down by bureaucracy. There are a handful of grant-giving organisations in the art world that support climate action, including some with specific grants dedicated to the cause (see Chapter 3). These, however, are often project-based and offer temporary support that can't be sustained unless institutions implement systemic change. When funding is available, the upfront costs for climate action can be significant, particularly when major overhauls to infrastructure, like new heating, ventilation and air-conditioning (HVAC) systems, are required. However, investment in sustainable infrastructure now may reduce overall expenses in the future.

Many institutions accept donations or grants, both in relation to sustainability projects and general operations. These donations can be complicated. Grants from governments and corporations can have stipulations in how they are used, as well as limitations – such as the duration of time the funds are available – that make it impossible, indeed unsustainable, to rely upon them, and they can 'too often come with the imperative that uncomfortable topics be checked at the door', notes culture and sustainability specialist Douglas Worts.[29] Institutions must also grapple with the public perception of their donations, as accepting funds can be considered an alignment with the donor's politics and actions. Several museums worldwide have been or are currently funded by major oil companies, relationships that have spurred significant protests and acts of vandalism (see Chapter 2). In the UK, the Tate museums were sponsored by BP for 26 years, cutting ties in 2017. The oil and gas company also has a long relationship with the British Museum in London, which in 2023 announced a new ten-year deal following the expiration of a 27-year partnership months earlier, a decision that sparked backlash. The Science Museum in London drew heavy criticism for its 2021 *Our Future Planet* exhibition, which was sponsored by oil and gas giant Shell. In June 2024 the Science Museum announced it had cut ties with the oil company Equinor for failing to reduce its carbon emissions to align with the Paris Accord. While the museum pats itself on the back for this separation, it still retains ties to BP and Adani Group, a major Indian coal company.

In the United States the Museum of Modern Art, New York (MoMA) faces ongoing demonstrations for its relationship with Henry Kravis and Marie-Josée Kravis, who have donated millions to the institution (Marie-Josée is also Chair of its board), due to the ties of Henry's investment firm KKR with the fossil fuel industry. In Texas the Museum of Fine Arts, Houston boasts a stunning Nancy and Rich Kinder Building named after the museum patrons whose multibillion-dollar fortune was amassed primarily through Rich's role as co-founder and executive chairman of Kinder Morgan, the energy giant that is one of the largest energy-infrastructure organisations in North America. (While Kinder Morgan has faced controversy and backlash for pipeline projects at various points, the museum has received little criticism for its connection with the Kinders, perhaps a result of the long oil legacy in Texas.)

For some institutions, fossil fuel connections are ingrained in their DNA. MoMA, for example, was co-founded by Abby Aldrich Rockefeller, daughter-in-law of Standard Oil founder John D. Rockefeller. Similarly, the J. Paul Getty Trust established a world-class group of museums and research and conservation centres in Los Angeles with funds from the Getty Oil Company founder J. Paul Getty. Likewise, the National Gallery of Art in Washington, DC was founded by industrialist Andrew Mellon. These are just a handful of examples of the ties between the art and fossil fuel industries, some of which are inextricably linked to the institutions and some, like the Getty, are involved with many climate initiatives, from organising exhibitions to funding climate action. Similarly, Mellon's philanthropy has trickled across generations, nations and industries, mainly through the Andrew W. Mellon Foundation, the esteemed grant-giving organisation founded by his children in 1969.

Increasingly, these partnerships have called into question the ethics of the cultural institutions that accept the funds. One argument is that the institutions sponsored by companies in the fossil fuel industry might not be inclined to implement systems that use renewable energy. These partnerships can also lead to 'artwashing', a term describing the use of art to improve the image of organisations engaging in acts that are detrimental to the environment. ('Artwashing' can also apply to issues beyond the climate crisis, such as partnerships between art institutions and businesses that directly or indirectly fund war.) Ultimately, the issue of funding is complex. Organisations need funds to survive, but if the sources of their funds are contributing to climate change, does their survival outweigh that of the environment? As we'll see in the next chapter, there's no art on a dead planet.

If step one is identifying the issues of sustainability in the art world and step two is overcoming roadblocks, step three is knowing what to do with the information. For many individuals and institutions, this involves creating a climate-action plan, which can be a formal, written plan, or more of a general ethos to take steps towards a greener future. This is where the network of climate organisations and collectives has become not only useful, but integral, particularly when it comes to information-sharing and crowdsourcing of resources and expertise. Chapter 3 will dive deeper into the work these groups have done and the climate actions they've supported. First, it's necessary to discuss the most important part of the art world: artists and the work they make.

2

Art and Artists Become Catalysts for Change

In our complex modern society, we are faced daily with a barrage of concerns. It's overwhelming to exist in a world full of climate disasters, war, bigotry, violence and constant threats to bodily autonomy. An individual person can only do so much to understand and address the increasingly urgent issues of the day. Art, however, can act as a catalyst for change. It can evoke empathy and make issues more relatable, science more digestible and hard topics more palatable, thus welcoming audiences to better understand them. It can open pathways to form creative solutions and rethink the systems that define our lives. In the fight against climate change, the role of art and artists is crucial.

This chapter will highlight some of the artists at the forefront of climate action. This form of activism is two-fold and relates both to the content the artist is creating and to the operations of their studio practice. The former is straightforward – artists leveraging their platform to educate and inspire change. The latter – artists maintaining studio practices where climate-conscious decisions are the norm and striving to hold partnering organisations accountable to do the same – happens behind the scenes. This chapter also touches on protests, a topic that I have been surprised to find is what people often imagine when I say climate action in the art world, perhaps because of the theatrics of the events and the amount of coverage they receive in the media. Art and art institutions have become tools and venues for protests, as well as the subjects of protests, and I offer examples of both, as well as discussing how institutions have responded to them.

This chapter was undoubtedly the most difficult to write, as there are many talented artists engaging with climate action, all of whom deserve attention. Moreover, the intersectional nature of climate justice means that artists who do not address the topic from a climate-first standpoint (and instead focus on social justice and racial equality, for example) are also contributing valuable expertise to the conversation. Because I can't feature all of them, I've tried to highlight the work of artists who approach climate action in different ways and at different scales to illustrate how diverse the entryways to sustainability and climate action are and, I hope, inspire a broad audience to see how their own lives might relate to the issues.

As a formal movement in art history, Environmental Art began 60 to 70 years ago. Broadly speaking, in the postwar years of the 20th century, art increasingly became a tool for all kinds of activism as artists aired their grievances against war and contemporary politics. This coincided with significant milestones in environmentalism, including Rachel Carson's pioneering book *Silent Spring* (1962), which documented the environmental impact of chemical pesticides. The first Earth Day in the US was celebrated in 1970, and the United Nations Environment Programme's annual World Environment Day began in 1973. In the 1970s slogans like 'only one Earth' and topics of greenhouse gases, ecology and global warming trickled into mainstream conversation.

Environmental Art emerged amidst this background and at a time when artists began to think about humans' relationship with the natural world. One of the pioneers of the movement is the Hungarian American artist Agnes Denes. Among her most influential pieces is *Wheatfield – A Confrontation: Battery Park Landfill, Downtown Manhattan* (1982), for which she planted a two-acre wheatfield in a landfill site in lower Manhattan, New York, and cultivated a stunning expanse of golden wheat. The ephemeral field and subsequent photographs of the project acted as a symbol of agriculture and sustenance lying just blocks from Wall Street, itself a symbol of power, inequality and greed, sentiments heightened in the recession years of the 1980s. The harvested wheat was then exhibited in *The International Art Show for the End of World Hunger*, which was organised by the Minnesota Museum of Art and travelled to nearly 30 cities across the world from 1987 to 1990, reflecting the global nature of the issues Denes addressed. Denes has reimagined this piece four times to date, nearly always choosing a location of high real-estate value, including a version created in June 2024 with Tinworks Art, a non-profit art space in Bozeman, Montana, a city that has become increasingly expensive due to an influx of out-of-state buyers. The concerns for the intertwined nature of environmental and social issues that existed when Denes first undertook the project are just as relevant today.

As Environmental Art emerged, so too did Land Art, which saw artists in the 1960s and 1970s rethink the institutional art model centred on the white cube and create works with and on the land. There is something of a chicken-and-egg relationship between Environmental Art and Land Art, sometimes called Earth Art, and there is often overlap. Land Art, though using land and earth as subject and material, is not always created with an environmental, social or activist agenda, whereas Environmental Art takes these as its impetus. The Environmental and Land Art genres sowed seeds for some of the issues at the intersection of art and climate action that we still grapple with today. As described by one of the seminal books on the subject: 'The decade of the 1960s that spawned Land Art was a period of longing – for a future that broke with a complacent present and for a past that transcended both'.[1] This message still resonates. As the repercussions of climate change become more urgent, even something as simple as a beautiful landscape can present an opportunity to discuss what is at risk.

Art and Artists as Catalysts for Education and Change Today

Today, we are reaching the point of climate breakdown, and we cannot survive by sustaining the status quo. The planet will survive, human and non-human species will not. For us to survive, we need to find solutions that foreground resiliency, remediation and regeneration. Regeneration can't undo the damage entirely, but it can help repair and restore natural ecosystems. Regenerative art projects, in my opinion, are some of the most exciting and promising forms of climate action.

One such example is a public installation by Jordan Weber. Entitled *Detroit Remediation Forest* (2024), the project aims to purify the polluted air of East Canfield, a predominately Black community in Detroit, Michigan, and to arm locals with knowledge. In creating the work, Weber collaborated with the non-profit organisations Sidewalk Detroit and Canfield Consortium to plant air-purifying trees and other plant species in a public park in East Canfield, actively helping to clean the air. In addition, Weber installed a giant, golden sculpture in the shape of two overlapping African crowns. Where the crowns' jewels might be, Weber placed air-quality sensors that glow depending on the readings of nearby monitors, thus arming residents with knowledge about their own air. The installation couldn't be more urgent. In 2024 the American Lung Association's 'State of the Air' report named Detroit the 13th worst metro area in the US for annual pollution. The report, which 'grades exposure to unhealthy levels of ground-level ozone air pollution, annual particle pollution and short-term spikes in particle pollution over a three-year period',[2] puts a quantifiable assessment to what locals have been reporting for years. In East Canfield, the smell of fumes from the massive Stellantis-Mack car manufacturing plant – a site that engenders constant air-quality violations – chokes the air several blocks away, something I experienced first-hand in May 2024.[3] Weber's project provides residents with a green space that will hopefully offer some respite from the polluted air.[4]

Studies illustrate the impact of air pollutants on the heating and cooling of the planet, as well as the effect climate change has on air quality – the two exacerbate one another.[5] Weber's installation points to one of the forms of climate activism that artists are best poised to undertake: giving visual representations to the invisible causes of climate change. This was also the topic of a group show at the Blanton

Museum of Art at the University of Texas, Austin in 2023–4. Curated by climate writer Jeff Goodell, the exhibition, *If the Sky Were Orange: Art in the Time of Climate Change*, took inspiration from a comment a scientist made to Goodell almost twenty years prior: that if greenhouse gases changed the colour of the sky, we'd be more aware of their presence.[6] The show examined hundreds of years of artists engaging with the environment, illustrating how humans impacted the world around us generations before we understood the consequences. The exhibition took on greater significance as it coincidentally opened just a few months after skies across much of the US turned orange due to rampant wildfires in Canada, an unprecedented sight in many of the places affected, though some states experienced this again in 2024, a harrowing sign of a 'new norm'. For its exhibition *Our Ecology: Toward a Planetary Living*, also in 2023–4, the Mori Art Museum in Tokyo staged a similar exploration of humans' impact on the climate, illustrating how artists throughout history have raised awareness of environmental damage. The museum also took efforts to reduce the carbon footprint and waste in staging the show, minimising shipping and prioritising recyclable materials.

In these examples, the consequences of human activity and the causes of climate change are front and centre. They also beg the question of what we're going to do about it. We know climate change is causing glaciers to melt, sea levels to rise, air and water quality to deteriorate and heat to stifle entire communities. In East Canfield, residents I spoke with said they had tried to ignore the polluted air in their neighbourhood, as it was one of many issues of environmental racism they face; the predominately Black community has experienced displacement for generations – including for the complex that now houses the Stellantis-Mack plant – and live with a significant risk of flooding and poor water quality. Even when manufacturing plants like that affecting East Canfield do not displace citizens, their presence and expansions emit pollutants in the air, negatively impacting the residents' quality of life, yet the businesses often receive significant tax incentives.[7] Air pollution is particularly harmful, with reports in recent years showing that Black residents of Detroit are three times more likely to be hospitalised for asthma than white people.[8] Weber's installation allows residents to confront this and gives them the tools to advocate for clean air.

In Texas, where the Blanton Museum show took place, the history of oil extraction and energy production is a point of pride. However, the state is also a leader in renewable energy, providing the US with approximately 16 per cent of its entire electricity generated from renewable sources. Texas has the US's highest utility-scale, wind-powered energy generation and the second-highest generation of solar-powered energy.[9] Exhibitions like *If the Sky Were Orange* are crucial in educating communities so intertwined with fossil fuels about the benefits of renewable energy. Jeff Goodell was careful not to patronise or isolate the museum's local audience. Instead, he carefully selected works that clearly illustrated the climate issues at hand, as well as the activities and industries that cause them, letting viewers decide whether or not they would choose to see what was in front of them. If they did take the bait, they could easily access information on climate change and activism in the library of books Goodell included for visitors to read.

These examples illustrate the hard-to-see causes of climate change, while other artworks and artists focus on its effects. One famous example is Olafur Eliasson's *Ice Watch*, a series he began in 2014 and has repeated twice to coincide with major climate-change policy and awareness events. Created with geologist Minik Rosing, *Ice Watch* features giant blocks of ice detached from an ice sheet along the Nuup Kangerlua fjord in Greenland, which the team transported and installed outside specific locations. For the first iteration of *Ice Watch*, Eliasson and Rosing installed the ice blocks outside City Hall in Copenhagen in 2014 to coincide with the publication of the UN Fifth Assessment Report on Climate Change. The second installment was near the Place du Panthéon in Paris during the 2015 COP 21 talks that resulted in the Paris Accord. For the third version, the team installed 24 blocks outside Tate Modern in London in 2018, coinciding with the COP 24 talks in Poland. Each of the behemoth blocks weighed between 1.5 and 5 tons and slowly melted in front of visitors' eyes. As a description of the project on the museum's website states, 'Although we may have seen photographs of the melting ice caps, we rarely have a physical experience of these conditions'.[10]

As an installation that directly speaks to environmental issues, *Ice Watch* was subjected to scrutiny from the public and media concerned with the carbon footprint of bringing the ice to London.[11] This alone is worth noting as an example of how influential the project was. If the public is concerned about the carbon emissions of *Ice Watch*, they should be concerned with all such impacts from every institution for every exhibition, always. *Ice Watch* sparked conversations that should become a normal part of the art world's operations. As is common in his practice, Eliasson's studio carried out a carbon-footprint report, in collaboration with Julie's Bicycle, that determined the total carbon emissions of bringing the blocks of ice from Greenland was 55 metric tons of CO_2, equivalent to 52 people flying from London to Greenland and back to see the ice melting first-hand. In a blog post on Julie's Bicycle's website, an unnamed author wrote, 'The last time we worked on *Ice Watch* was for the Paris edition . . . Then public interest in the carbon footprint of the work was small. But since then, public awareness on climate has shifted dramatically.'[12] *Ice Watch* had become a barometer for the public's concern for carbon emissions.

Bringing the ice blocks to Tate Modern, where their slow dissolution could be seen by thousands of museumgoers and passersby alike, undoubtedly created a smaller carbon footprint than if each viewer had flown to see the melting glaciers in person. This was also an argument used to validate Christie's 2017 world tour of Leonardo da Vinci's *Salvator Mundi*. Everything we do has a carbon footprint: it's the intentions and impact behind this expenditure that matter. *Ice Watch* is still referenced as one of the most memorable examples of an artwork engaging with the climate crisis for its ability to spark crucial conversations, and I would argue one of the most impactful. It should also be noted that Eliasson's studio made donations to the UK's woodland conservation charity, the Woodland Trust, to offset more than the emissions of the London installation.[13]

While *Ice Watch* helps people to see the effects of climate change, artists also ask viewers to consider the world from the perspective of non-human species. Tomás Saraceno's 2022 exhibition *Particular Matter(s)* at The Shed in New York took on this very mission. Shifting the human-centric viewpoint of ecology, Saraceno challenged viewers to rethink an often disliked and feared member of the animal kingdom: spiders. In the first part of the show, visitors walked through a dark room containing large glass vitrines, inside which were giant, stunningly intricate and delicate spider webs. Exiting this gallery, visitors then encountered another dark space that was empty apart from a large raking light that streaked across the room and highlighted the particulate matter in the air. Visitors had to walk through the dusty, dirty air to continue through the show. Of course, the air is the same throughout the building and visitors breathe particulate matter whether or not they're aware of it.

After first viewing the spider webs and then being forced to confront all the dust and dirt that floats around us (and all species) constantly, viewers then experienced a dramatic shift in perspective as the exhibition culminated in an immersive sensory installation. To experience the piece *Free the Air: How to hear the universe in a spider/web* (2022), visitors walked onto one of two platforms, elevated at 12 and 40 feet above the ground, that opened into a bright white, dome-shaped room. Attached to each platform were massive steel and wire nets. As people walked onto the nets, they dipped as if on a trampoline and continued to move as the weight of others shifted the net. I chose the 40-foot-high net from which the lower one was visible, its visitors spread out across the surface. After a few minutes, we were instructed to sit or lie down. Hazy air filled the room and the lights dimmed to near pitch-darkness while an eight-minute, sub-sonic performance vibrated through the metal nets. Created from recordings of the movement of the Earth, air particles and spiderwebs, the vibrations allowed us to feel the world from the perspective of a spider. Bringing the interconnectedness of all species to the fore, Saraceno beautifully argues for the importance of considering not just our own wellbeing, but that of every being on the planet.[14]

Then there are artists who focus on the planet itself, celebrating Earth and lamenting natural destruction by highlighting extraction, colonisation, displacement and land rights in their work. One such project is Shayla Blatchford's *The Anti-Uranium Mapping Project* (2023 ongoing), an interactive storytelling website and exhibition that examines the impact of uranium mining on Navajo Nation land. Taking the form of a map with personal stories and accounts from community members, as well as miners and environmental lawyers, the work seeks to bring together the Navajo community and educate viewers on the history of uranium mining and its possible future with uranium's potential use in nuclear-powered energy. Blatchford hopes the project can bolster tribal sovereignty and empower the Navajo community with tools to make decisions about the uranium mining sites as the demands on energy solutions evolve.[15]

In August 2024 *The Anti-Uranium Mapping Project* was one of 19 works selected to receive the Anonymous Was A Woman Environmental Art Grants, a climate-specific grant from Anonymous Was A Woman and The New York Foundation for the Arts (NYFA) that awards women-identifying artists with up to US$20,000 to support environmental art projects.[16] Launched in 2022, the grant will distribute a total of US$250,000 to projects that engage with environmental concerns through a range of themes, including regeneration, decolonisation and ecofeminism, and inspire thought and public engagement. In addition to this climate-specific grant, both NYFA and Anonymous Was A Woman support the arts in a number of ways, with NYFA providing resources such as fiscal sponsorship, career advice, and grants and awards to individuals and organisations, while Anonymous Was A Woman has provided unrestricted grants of US$25,000 to ten women-identifying artists over the age of 40 each year (with the exception of the environmental grants, which do not have this age requirement). In November 2024 it increased the number of recipients to 15 and the grants to US$50,000.

Artists Take Action in the Studio

These examples of artists engaging with climate content illustrate how art can be mobilised to educate the public on environmental issues and support broader pushes to understand and address the climate crisis. Another crucial way artists are foregrounding climate action is by improving their own practices.

Olafur Eliasson's studio is also worth studying for its sustainable operations and climate activism. In addition to *Ice Watch*, Eliasson is known for a range of sculptures, installations, architectural projects, food initiatives and collective activism, including the *Little Sun* products – small, portable, solar-powered lights designed with engineer Frederik Ottesen in 2012 that were first created to bring light to people in Ethiopia living without electricity. The project has since expanded to include larger and different designs available for purchase online and in major cultural institutions like MoMA and Tate Modern. Proceeds fund *Little Sun*'s philanthropic work, including providing power for agriculture, education and health infrastructures and systems in Sub-Saharan African communities without electricity.

Environmental and ecological concerns have been at the heart of Eliasson's practice, directly and indirectly, for decades. In 2020 his studio published the essay 'Fourteen Views of Studio Olafur Eliasson's Sustainability Agenda, 2020', in the exhibition catalogue for *Olafur Eliasson: Sometimes the river is the bridge* at the Museum of Contemporary Art, Tokyo.[17] In it, Eliasson and thirteen others from the studio discussed how they were working to implement sustainable operations in general and, in particular, for the artist's participation in an international exhibition. Among their concerns at the time were the need for sustainable packing solutions, the carbon footprint of travel and whether shipping companies could use new energy (sources alternative to fossil fuels). In the text, artwork coordinator Kajana Wagner recounted a conversation with shippers Hasenkamp after asking about new energy: 'I asked Hasenkamp, our main shipping partner, "Do you get a lot of requests like this?" And they said we actually were the first ones to ask . . . We, as the studio can say, "If you want this exhibition, we have to calculate two months for shipping because we are not going to fly it." But you cannot transition immediately to doing everything at once . . . we are pushing as much as we can. But it's not in our hands alone."[18] Wagner's comments are an important reminder that everyone in the industry has agency, including artists, collectors and institutions worldwide. Supporting industries might make changes on their own, but the more their clients ask for green options, the more these services will need to be provided.

Recognising this agency and understanding how to ask partners and vendors to implement sustainable practices can be challenging for artists and all individuals within the industry. To this end, in the spring of 2021, the worker-led collective Galleries Commit (see Chapter 3) launched an artist-led endeavour called Artists Commit. The group helps members stay accountable, shares best practice and encourages artists to advocate for sustainability and climate actions in the institutions they work with. 'Artists Commit formed in order to activate the commitment we signed with Galleries Commit, and to catalyze our collective power', Artists Commit founding member Robin F. Williams told me upon announcing the group in 2021. 'By coordinating, we hold each other accountable, and also encourage the galleries and institutions we work with to address the climate crisis. By providing resources like climate-action plans, we are empowering artists to support each other and to make change together.'[19]

Since its launch, over 300 artists have signed the pledge on Artists Commit's website, which includes a statement on the overlap between the climate crisis and racial, social, economic and labour injustices, as imbalance in one system is often both a cause and an effect of imbalance in another. Several declarants have also worked with the group to create Climate Impact Reports (CIRs) – which can be completed via a user-friendly online form – to calculate and analyse the carbon footprint and waste of an exhibition, among other things. Artists Commit also offers mentorship to start, guide and complete the reports, as well as the option of receiving small stipends. The mentorship programme was initially sponsored by Teiger Foundation, a grant-giving organisation that supports several climate initiatives (see Chapter 3).

Climate Impact Reports help artists and the institutions they work with to understand what questions might need to be asked to execute an exhibition sustainably and how to solve the problems often encountered. The reports are shared online, so anyone hoping to tackle their own issues can read about similar experiences. The more reports are conducted, the better equipped artists will be to operate sustainably. Such reporting is also useful for supporting industries and vendors, like shipping and packaging suppliers, to anticipate future needs as sustainable options become the norm.

One of the first reports was created for Williams's 2021 exhibition *Out Lookers* at PPOW contemporary art gallery in New York. The show featured large-scale paintings of supernatural female figures made with a variety of techniques, such as airbrush, marbling, oil and staining. The show considered how women are portrayed in American media as scapegoats (like the final girl trope in horror films, in which a female protagonist endures and witnesses violence for the duration of the film and confronts the villain in the end), as well as derogatory terms like 'trolls' and potentially evil, mistrusted figures like witches and ghosts. Williams aimed to draw attention to the mistreatment of women and non-binary identities, relating this to the destruction of the planet.

Out Lookers marked PPOW's first carbon-conscious exhibition. Williams's CIR includes an outline of their studio's climate policy in three categories: cutting emissions, eliminating waste and supporting people. To cut emissions, Williams limits their own actions, for example by reducing plane travel, not travelling to art fairs and only participating in local lectures. They also set limitations for their collectors, stating that, 'Non-local collectors who buy work in advance of exhibitions must wait to receive work until after [the] exhibition', and 'placement of artwork in art fairs should be given local priority'.[20] Williams's consideration of their collectors' actions is significant. It's one thing to hold yourself accountable, but to have system-wide change, we must hold all parties accountable. Taking collectors into consideration represents one of the next important steps towards a greener future (see Chapter 4).

In the second part of Williams's studio climate policy, they address waste elimination with straightforward steps that include reusing materials, offering surplus materials to others and reducing or reusing plastics. The third part, supporting people, points to the intersectional nature of climate action and includes paying fair wages, only partnering with organisations that employ or represent people from a wide range of races, ethnicities, genders and sexual orientations, and donating to climate and/or social justice groups. The CIR also outlines the gallery's climate commitment, which centres a similar ethos and includes shifts to LED lighting and clean energy. To understand the impact of *Out Lookers*, the CIR evaluates the carbon emissions from powering the gallery, shipping the artworks (totalling just seven road trips from the artist's studio in Brooklyn and local lenders), packaging (also done consciously for minimal waste) and printing for the catalogue and publicity materials (the gallery encouraged the use of QR codes for checklists and press releases and only printed two physical copies for the front desk). The report also highlights materials that could not be recycled (paper and plastic tape, and Magic Erasers, for example), and includes notes about how the artist and gallery would use *Out Lookers* as a case study for climate-conscious decisions in the future. The total carbon emissions for the exhibition were 1.3 metric tons CO_2 (for context, the average car in the US produces 1 metric ton CO_2 every three months,[21] and the average carbon footprint for an American person is approximately 16 metric tons CO_2 per year[22]). Such reporting is still nascent and it's difficult to compare exhibitions for a number of reasons: the size of the show, whether the artist and artworks were local to the exhibition space, the discipline (a Richard Serra sculpture would undoubtedly have a larger carbon footprint to ship and install than a Serra drawing, for example), as well as the level of detail in the report itself. Even within the completed CIRs, there is inconsistency in how many factors the artist or institution conducting the report was able to track. Over time, direct comparisons of carbon emissions and CIRs between exhibitions will be useful, but more data and analysis are needed. Like many other climate actions, Williams's exhibition included a donation to permanent, old-growth land conservation through Art into Acres, an artist-founded non-profit that supports land conservation through monetary donations and the sale of artworks (see Chapter 3).

In July 2024 GCC launched a similar initiative to Artists Commit called the Artist Toolkit. Also sponsored by Teiger Foundation, the toolkit empowers artists to adopt best practices across ten areas, including activism, materials, shipping and packaging, and exhibition display. The toolkit includes case studies of artists who have implemented sustainable practices, and templates and guidelines for things like decarbonising finances (essentially removing or excluding investments with fossil fuel companies from daily banking and staff pensions, and avoiding working with high-carbon banks) and what to ask suppliers to ensure their operations and services are socio-environmentally responsible. Like Artists Commit, GCC's Artist Toolkit also supports artists to advocate for best practices within their partner organisations through an environmental responsibility rider, a document similar to Robin F. Williams's studio climate policy that outlines the sustainability expectations between collaborators, such as between an artist and a gallery, to understand climate targets.

No Art on a Dead Planet

On the topic of climate action in the art world, it's impossible not to discuss the role of art and art institutions as both tools for and targets of protests. As tools, creating art for protests has a long, rich history with countless examples. In Paris in 1968, students began demonstrating against the nation's university system, using hundreds of posters to disseminate their messages. In 1987, during the AIDS epidemic in the US, six men (Avram Finkelstein, Brian Howard, Oliver Johnston, Charles Kreloff, Chris Lione and Jorge Socarrás) developed the now iconic poster of a hot pink, inverted triangle set against a black backdrop with the words 'Silence = Death'. The image was used to protest the US government's inaction (and homophobia) and is a significant cultural reference still used today.

Before we had the terminology to define climate change, environmentalist and artist Robert Rauschenberg created a poster of a bald eagle surrounded by images of detritus, an endangered gorilla and polluted waterways for the first ever Earth Day on 22 April 1970. More recently, Greta Thunberg's famous placard reading 'skolstrejk för klimatet' (school strike for climate) has accompanied the activist's ongoing global school strikes since August 2018, the sparse, white poster with black writing now symbolising youth activism. In Maine, the collective Artists' Rapid Response Team (ARRT!) creates eye-catching, socially engaged banners, posters and props for groups promoting social change. AART! has worked with over 60 non-profits to provide creative, impactful imagery that amplifies their messages, including fights for clean air, Indigenous sovereignty and clean energy, as well as social issues not related directly to the climate crisis. Beyond their use during protests, such posters and banners are tools to help spread messages online, giving organisations visual resources to leverage the global reach of social media.

While in these cases artists and activists purposefully made work to support a cause, it is increasingly common, if controversial, for art to be subverted as a target for protesters. Some of these protests have taken aim at the operations of the art institutions in which the works are located, and others have used museum settings to speak to broader environmental issues not necessarily tied to the museums themselves. Demonstrations reflecting the latter have been garnering remarkable traction in recent years. In some cases, activists unfurl banners, occupy galleries and disrupt events. In countless others, they've targeted artwork (though the art is typically unharmed). Perhaps the best-known group of climate activists undertaking these protests is Just Stop Oil, which made headlines in October 2022 (and again in September 2024) by throwing soup at Vincent van Gogh's painting *Sunflowers* (1888) on display at the National Gallery in London. Just Stop Oil has undertaken several similar events at other museums across the UK, including the Royal Academy of Arts in London. In most instances, the activists reveal concealed shirts that read 'Just Stop Oil' before throwing a substance over – or pasting fear-inspiring images onto – a work of art (often one related to nature) and then gluing themselves to its frame or to the floor nearby. Funded through donations and in major part by the California-based group Climate Emergency Fund, which supports environmental activists and counts as its co-founders Aileen Getty (oil tycoon J. Paul Getty's granddaughter), Just Stop Oil is one of several initiatives worldwide that partake in such displays of varying degrees of disruption.[23]

Examples of such protests abound. In January 2024 members of the activist group Riposte Alimentaire entered the Musée du Louvre in Paris and threw soup at Leonardo da Vinci's *Mona Lisa* (*c.*1503–19). In the US, similar protests have occurred, including the smearing of paint onto a vitrine containing Edgar Degas's *La petite danseuse de quatorze ans* (Little Dancer Aged Fourteen, 1880) at the National Gallery of Art in Washington, DC, an act undertaken by members of Declare Emergency. These incidents involving artwork nearly always result in the activists' arrests. In other cases, activists disrupt events: for example, Extinction Rebellion has staged protests at museums like the Guggenheim and the American Museum of Natural History, both in New York, and Tate Modern in London, as well as interrupting a sale at Christie's New York in November 2023. Not just targeting the art industry, Extinction Rebellion has also blocked highways and airports, dyed the canals of Venice green and interrupted live theatrical performances. These incidents where artwork is left untouched often result in the swift removal of the protesters, though some arrests do occur.

In these examples, activists use cultural institutions to raise issues of climate change and environmental issues more broadly, but other protesters are also targeting museums themselves. As discussed in Chapter 1, funding is a major issue across the art industry and many institutions accept financial support from people and companies with ties to the fossil fuel industry. These sponsorships are well known, making many of the art organisations the target of public scrutiny. What is interesting about these instances is how the institutions respond, if at all.

New York's MoMA sees periodic protests for its ties to the fossil fuel industry via donors Henry Kravis and Marie-Josée Kravis. Activists have targeted the museum on multiple occasions, including a February 2024 protest in which several climate groups entered the building during regular hours and unfurled a banner reading 'MoMA: Drop KKR', a reference to Henry Kravis's fossil fuel-connected private equity firm. They also wore shirts with the same message and chanted statements in a similar vein, calling out the museum for claiming its commitment to 'leadership in sustainability', as it states on its website.[24] The activists also distributed fake greeting cards with an image of a Roy Lichtenstein painting featuring a crying woman lamenting, 'Our planet is drowning! Why won't MoMA dump billionaire climate criminals?' Inside the card was information on KKR and a link to a petition for Marie-Josée's removal from the board. Museum security closed the area where the activists were protesting and briefly closed the museum.[25]

Protesters have also targeted MoMA during fundraising events with donors and supporters like the Kravises in attendance. At its 2024 Party in the Garden fundraiser, activists attended the after-party, linking arms and sitting on the dancefloor, their chants competing with the live musical performance. Rather than remove them, security let the protesters stay, keeping watch and taking their photos to document their identities, which eye-witnesses called a remarkable and surreal moment as attendees danced nearby trying their best to ignore the activists,[26] an image of which was published in *The New York Times* in a post-party report.[27] Perhaps even more surreal was the demonstration the year prior, which coincided with the devastating Canadian wildfires that turned skies across much of the north-eastern US orange, providing a smoky, apocalyptic backdrop. In response to this and most protests, MoMA typically has its security staff monitor the activities, sometimes with help from police, allowing them to run their course as long as business is not disrupted.[28] On occasion, arrests are made, including at a September 2023 protest when 16 activists attempted to occupy the building overnight.[29] For now, the protests at MoMA seem to have little apparent impact, but if other museums can serve as examples, persistence might be key to achieving a result.

In 2017 Tate ended its nearly 30-year partnership with the oil and gas giant BP following six years of protests and unsanctioned performances by activist groups such as Liberate Tate and Platform London across the museum's locations. Upon announcing the news, a BP spokesperson told the *Independent* that the decision was not related to the protests, possibly an attempt to prevent similar actions.[30] Correlation may not prove causation, but even addressing the issues of the protests points to their impact. Perhaps London's British Museum should take note. Though the museum has been the subject of protests for several years for its long-standing partnership with BP, this partnership, as I mentioned in Chapter 1, was renewed with a ten-year contract in 2023 after its controversial, nearly three-decade sponsorship deal had ended just months earlier.

While the British Museum is doubling down, success stories similar to the Tate's have been seen in the Netherlands. In May 2017, after targeting the institution on previous occasions, seven activists from Fossil Free Culture staged a performance inside the Van Gogh Museum in Amsterdam, drinking a dark liquid from large, white scallop shells. Indigestible, the liquid spilled from their mouths onto their pristine white dresses and down to the floor of the museum. Titled *Drop the Shell, from Prestige to Disgrace* (2017), the performance called into question the nearly two-decade sponsorship between the Van Gogh Museum and the oil and gas company Shell. Additional activist groups followed this act of 'disobedient art' as Fossil Free Culture calls its work,[31] and the museum and Shell stated they had mutually agreed to end their relationship in 2018.[32] At the same time, the Mauritshuis in The Hague ended a six-year contract with Shell in what was also called a mutual decision. However, the museum's annual reports revealed its financial dependence upon the support from the oil company and two other partners, funds considered 'crucial for the long-term future of the museum', indicating the significance of their separation and the widespread financial impact of mounting pressure to cut fossil fuel ties.[33]

Whether for protests or to amplify issues of climate change, the role of art and artists in catalysing climate action is clear. The question now is how institutions are following suit, identifying areas where sustainable measures can be implemented, forming climate plans and translating these into action.

3

Climate Commitments Turn into Climate Action

Climate pledges are futile if they are not acted upon. In the art world and beyond, it will take years to identify and undo damaging practices and foster regenerative and sustainable ones, but we have to start somewhere. Efforts to overcome and mitigate the roadblocks and issues in the art world outlined in Chapter 1 have given rise to a wave of galleries, non-profits, art fairs and suppliers declaring their commitments to climate-conscious operations. Now we are seeing a broader push to turn these commitments into action with the help of climate specialists and collectives. This chapter explores some of the climate actions that have occurred since 2020 to improve individual operations and address issues with industry-wide impact. Many other examples exist, and many more are still to come.

Pre-Pandemic Institutional Climate Action

The role of museums in our complex 21st-century society is a topic ripe for debate that can fill entire books. Museums can amplify social issues and educate on solutions. In regard to the climate crisis, museums are uniquely positioned to act as models for a greener future. As art and climate consultant Laura Lupton[1] explains:

Museums are considered one of the most trustworthy sources in America, are active carbon emitters, are significant economic contributors, and are often community pillars. They can be climate influencers, carbon reducers, policy advocates, and climate resilience infrastructures and hubs. The risk for museums to not step into this role will be increasingly dire in the years to come, but the opportunity for culture leadership available now for those integrating climate at the heart of strategy is energizing and inspiring.[2]

Even before we entered the current state of enthusiasm for climate action – indeed, even before we had the language to talk about climate change – institutions were making decisions with what today we might call sustainability in mind. Dia Art Foundation was founded in New York City in 1974 on environmental principles that resonate today. 'Fifty years ago, our three founders (Philippa de Menil, Heiner Friedrich and Helen Winkler) established what they referred to as an "anti museum"', explains Dia Director Jessica Morgan. 'They had in mind not a building of bricks and mortar filled with objects but rather an institution built around the ambitions of artists.'[3] This ethos led Dia to support permanent works by artists outside of the institutional white cube, including Robert Smithson's *Spiral Jetty* (1970), an earthwork located on the shore of the Great Salt Lake in Utah. Consisting of over 6000 tons of black basalt rocks and earth, the monumental work extends into the water in a counterclockwise spiral (though with climate change and severe droughts, the water level often does not reach the piece).

'This commitment to permanent works was in opposition to the schedule of changing exhibitions and the shipment of art around the world for temporary exhibitions', Morgan adds. '[Dia's founders] thought specifically about resources and how these might be preserved.' Dia's shortest exhibition period is one year, longer than many museums and certainly longer than the breakneck speed of commercial galleries. Dia also exhibits work predominantly from its own collection or commissions projects on site to reduce shipping. Additionally, Dia Beacon and other sites under the foundation's stewardship are lit with daylight. The institution is also taking steps towards climate resilience, including its current landscape redesign of the Beacon campus, which will protect the buildings against rising water levels and floods.

Most organisations, however, were not founded with sustainability and climate education at the fore, but rather have adapted to implement best practices and incorporate environmental issues in their programming and exhibitions. Among pre-pandemic examples is the Charles H. Wright Museum of African American History in Detroit, Michigan, which has incorporated sustainable changes to its operations in a multi-level approach that encompasses several aspects, from its finances to education, visitor experience and exhibitions. In 2015, nearly a decade before other art institutions were beginning to address sustainability, The Wright, as it is known, created a full-time Chief Sustainability Officer position to develop a holistic climate-action plan for the museum and oversee the implementation of several initiatives, including efforts to increase recycling. The museum hosts ongoing programmes to address climate issues and engage and educate the local community, a crucial resource for Detroit in particular, as it and nearby communities have been affected by widespread environmental racism, such as the Flint water crisis. Often cited as an extreme example of the issue, Flint's water pollution began in 2014 when the city switched its drinking water from Detroit's system to the Flint River to save money, a decision that led to immediate health issues for residents in the predominately Black area because the water wasn't being treated for corrosion control. The subsequent illnesses (and 12 related deaths) from exposure to toxic lead and bacteria led to well-documented instances of political denial of the crisis.[4]

Not far after The Wright in pioneering institutional climate action is the UK's Tate, which in 2016 hired a full-time Environmental and Sustainability Manager to implement waste-management systems, research and incorporate new environmental operations, and train departments across the museum in sustainability initiatives. In 2019 the museum declared a climate emergency and created a Climate

Emergency Working Group of staff from across its locations. Tate also formed an interdepartmental Green Team and has taken several steps to implement sustainable operations institution-wide, such as energy-saving and waste-reducing initiatives like loosening its climate-control standards, switching to renewable energy in all galleries, limiting staff travel and installing solar panels. In 2023 Tate added a new Art and Ecology focus, hiring Marleen Boschen as adjunct curator. Prior to this position, Boschen was working towards her doctorate in cultural studies from Goldsmiths, where she specialised in the intersection of art and ecology, in particular the connected legacies of colonialism and extractive capitalism. Bringing this focus into her curatorial work at Tate, Boschen is helping the institution deepen its commitment to environmentalism and climate justice in its exhibition planning.[5]

It's not just major museum franchises like Tate that are devoting funds and resources to sustainability. The Horniman Museum and Gardens is an example of a smaller, more local London institution that released a climate and ecology manifesto in January 2020, outlining the institution's commitment to climate activism and sustainable operations. The Horniman has since undertaken several additional initiatives, including tracking and reporting its carbon footprint, embarking on water-reducing and reusing projects, and organising exhibitions and programming to educate the public on environmental issues and climate justice.[6] The chief executive of the Horniman, Nick Merriman, edited a useful book entitled *Museums and the Climate Crisis* (2024), which includes case studies of the issues museums are facing today because of climate change. Included in these is how to adapt infrastructures to ensure they operate sustainably in the future, and the role of the museum in reflecting urgent topics of the day and educating the public to encourage action.[7] A crucial resource for any museum worker (and arguably any visitor curious about the mission and responsibilities of these often publicly funded institutions), the book illuminates work being done behind the scenes at museums to address climate change.

A Green Wave: Post-Pandemic Climate Pledges Turn into Climate Action

For many institutions and individuals, becoming a member of groups like GCC and taking a climate pledge marked their first climate action. While GCC was formed with more of an industry-wide viewpoint, another group that launched at the onset of the pandemic began from the perspective of the worker. Called Galleries Commit, the collective started in a similar way to GCC with a group of gallery workers sharing their concerns over the climate crisis. They initially devised a multi-gallery curatorial project exploring how galleries and artists were adopting sustainable practices when displaying artwork, but with COVID-19 looming, Galleries Commit changed plans and wrote a letter committing to a climate-conscious future that was circulated among New York galleries on Earth Day 2020.[8] 'The worker-led aspect of the initiative lent us credibility while building a community on the ground that had direct insight into the primary blocks to climate action workers face, which then provided us the tools to leverage institutional change at the leadership level', says Laura Lupton, a co-founder of Galleries Commit.[9] The letter quickly attracted attention, with over 150 New York gallery workers from over 60 galleries signing the climate pledge alongside artists and other industry professionals.

Soon after the launch of Galleries Commit and GCC, as well as other groups across the US and Europe such as Art Switch, Art + Climate Action, and international chapters of GCC, a ripple effect of climate-consciousness started to spread across the art industry. In October of 2020 the Museum of Contemporary Art (MOCA) in Los Angeles announced the creation of an Environmental Council, the first for a major US art museum.[10] The Environmental Council supports environmentally focused exhibitions and programming and has helped the museum to work towards institution-wide carbon negativity and carbon-free energy. MOCA publicly states its full climate commitments, actions and goals on its website, updating the information as it continues to make changes. Such public statements and transparency regarding the actions underway were, and still are, becoming more common and are not just limited to the US and Europe. The National Gallery Singapore, for example, lists its detailed sustainability commitment on its website, including data on carbon-emission reports and steps taken for decarbonisation, such as installing solar panels.

Following the example of organisations like Tate and The Wright, institutions are also increasingly allocating funds for in-house sustainability positions, an important step to ensure long-term implementation of green measures. In April 2023 MOCA hired a full-time Environment and Sustainability Strategist to spearhead sustainability, climate action, and environmental-justice programming and exhibitions. Included in the exhibition programme is *Josh Kline: Climate Change* (June 2024 to January 2025). Kline's dystopian science-fiction installation imagines a world destroyed by climate change and illustrates how the people still living in a post-apocalyptic future might need to adapt to survive, giving a visual form to many of the hypotheticals that scientists warn of, such as entire cities being underwater. MOCA also hosts screenings of environmental films and talks with the filmmakers, as well as panels, lectures and performances with artists and activists.[11] This emphasis on environmental content is significant not only in establishing the museum as a trusted voice in the climate crisis, but it also demonstrates to all of its partners (artists, writers, activists etc.) that environmental issues are subjects worthy of a major institution's attention.

MOCA also undertakes climate action in the way it stages exhibitions, including *Pipilotti Rist: Big Heartedness, Be My Neighbor* (September 2021 to June 2022), the museum's first net-zero exhibition. MOCA considered sustainability at every step in organising the show, working with the artist's studio to track and mitigate the overall carbon footprint and reduce the show's climate impact. In an effort for transparency and information sharing, MOCA's Environmental Council co-founder and co-chair, Haley Mellin, conducted and published a Climate Impact Report for the exhibition, using Artists Commit's tool to thoroughly detail how the museum achieved the net-zero status for the show.[12] Included in the steps the museum and Rist took were sourcing local materials, shipping works by sea and land rather than air, and choosing a climate-conscious menu for the opening dinner. The report explains the waste associated with the show and how it was accounted for, including the reuse of crates, the repurposing of faux plants and props, and the recycling of drywall and carpeting. It also outlines the carbon footprint of the exhibition, computed with the assistance of GCC's calculator and considering numerous factors, such as flights and cars taken by the artist and her studio, shipping of artwork and the energy consumption in MOCA's Geffen building, where the exhibition took place. This final data point was informed by previous energy and utility usage to estimate the carbon footprint of the building, as the report was conducted during the run of the exhibition. The total carbon emissions for the show were 81.49+ metric tons CO_2 equivalent, and the museum double-offset its emissions by supporting carbon sequestration in Borneo and Peru. Importantly, the report also notes areas where the museum could not access carbon-emissions data, such as staff commutes, visitor travel and events. This final detail is significant in understanding that sustainability and climate action are evolving and that there will always be room for improvement.[13]

More recently, for their autumn 2024 exhibitions in partnership with the Getty's PST ART initiative, MOCA and the Hammer Museum, also in Los Angeles, piloted expanded climate-control parameters based on the Bizot Green Protocol, a set of guidelines published in 2015 by the Bizot Group (an influential, international group of museum leaders) that outline early concerns for the art industry's impact on the environment, focusing on energy reduction and institutional adaptability. In 2023 the group updated its Green Protocol with new suggestions for travel and, particularly noteworthy, wider climate-control parameters that allow for relative humidity and temperature and acknowledge the outdated nature of strict, all-encompassing guidelines. Under new standards, the group suggests that climate-control settings be considerate of the sensitivity of an object, so that less fragile or sensitive materials can be kept in less stringent, less energy-consuming environments. The standards, the group argues, should be flexible and based on the needs of an object, not on blanket requirements. This flexibility extends to the protocols themselves, with the Bizot Group declaring its commitment to reevaluate its guidelines every five years.[14]

MOCA and the Hammer's adoption of new Bizot standards was an initiative taken under the umbrella of the Getty's Climate Impact Program (CIP), which launched in 2023 to coincide with the PST ART programme *Art & Science Collide*. Developed with the guidance of consultant Laura Lupton and the artist Debra Scacco, the CIP encourages climate action among the over 60 organisations across Southern California that participated in PST ART. Other examples of action taken through the CIP include efforts by The Huntington in San Marino, California, and Fulcrum Arts in Pasadena to design their exhibitions with green practices, such as reusing materials, in mind. Lupton and Scacco also facilitated workshops and assisted institutions in creating Climate Impact Reports for their exhibitions to develop deeper analysis of the individual and collective impact of the PST ART programme. These initiatives will undoubtedly offer valuable case studies in climate action for Southern California's art industry.

In New York similar actions are underway at the Guggenheim, which created the role of Associate Director of Sustainability in February 2023 to lead its Green Team, an interdepartmental group of employees that works to establish iterative, holistic and collective sustainability strategies, joining ongoing efforts to implement sustainable operations at all its locations worldwide. For example, the Guggenheim Bilbao, in Spain, enacted a Sustainability Action Plan in 2022 to align operations with the UN General Assembly and achieve carbon neutrality by 2030. The museum updated this plan in 2023 after relaxing its climate-control standards in the fall of 2022.[15] The museum shares its plan, actions and future goals on its website. Like MOCA, the Guggenheim conducted a carbon-emissions report for its exhibition *Cecilia Vicuña: Spin Spin Triangulene* (May to September 2022). Also using GCC's carbon calculator, as well as that of Sustainability Tools in Cultural Heritage, the report was produced by Mellin and her non-profit, Art into Acres (discussed later in this chapter). As with MOCA's report, the Guggenheim's carbon calculation thoroughly details the methodology used and notes a similar caveat that visitor travel, events and utilities were not included in the calculation, allowing others to use it as a model. The report also warns that COVID-19 travel restrictions reduced travel and shipping for the exhibition, thus lowering the overall emissions. The total carbon emissions were 18.69 metric tons CO_2 equivalent. Based on this calculation, the museum made donations to Art into Acres to support the creation of Cape Froward National Park in southern Chile.

In an innovative effort to address its energy consumption and the broader shifts in energy production, in 2024 the Institute of Contemporary Art (ICA) Miami entered a five-year agreement with a subsidiary of ENGIE North America, a global energy company that specialises in low-carbon energy and services. Through the agreement, the ICA will procure Renewable Energy Certificates (RECs) for its energy consumption.[16] RECs essentially track and authenticate that energy is from a clean, renewable source.[17] This initiative continues the ICA's sustainability efforts, which include donating to land conservation with Art into Acres and The Florida Audubon Society. The museum has also conducted several carbon calculations and does carbon offsets (more on carbon offsets later in this chapter). From the carbon calculations, the ICA has made changes to its operations and activities, including procuring the RECs, as well as altering its shipping standards to ensure best practices are always undertaken. The museum also launched an Innovation Committee in 2021 to propose long-term plans for sustainability, including decarbonisation.

In 2021 the Indigenous cultural institution Forge Project was founded in Taghkanic, New York, to support Indigenous art and culture and to further decolonial efforts and education. The organisation, which transitioned into a non-profit in April 2024, hosts classes and artists-in-residence, has a lending collection of over 200 works by Indigenous artists, and has supported several artists' projects and performances. One of its main initiatives is a land-remediation project that began in 2022 and uses Indigenous knowledge to support a balanced plant ecosystem. Serving as a model for Indigenous futures, Land Back and rematriation, the remediation project includes fostering a meadow with native wildlife and plants and creating outdoor spaces for teaching Indigenous traditions and histories.[18] Rematriation (as opposed to repatriation) is a concept based on matrilineal societies and seeks to restore relationships between Indigenous peoples and their ancestral lands – a restoration of balance rather than an extractive process associated with patriarchy.[19]

Galleries Take Action

While museums have to adhere to certain standards, such as those set by the International Council of Museums (ICOM), whose members must heed its dictate that museums include diversity and sustainability as performance criteria, commercial galleries are afforded greater operational freedom. Indeed, without the need to serve the public and with a greater focus on financial gain, we might not be surprised were commercial galleries to be less involved with climate action. Thankfully, several galleries are dispelling this assumption, including global powerhouse Hauser & Wirth, which offers a valuable case study in how an institution can weave sustainability and climate-conscious operations into its DNA across multiple locations. Cliodhna Murphy, Hauser & Wirth's Global Head of Environmental Sustainability, began putting together data for the gallery's scopes 1 and 2 emissions report in 2019. At the time, she was the Director of Operations in London and was considering several elements of the gallery's climate impact, exploring things like divesting pension funds away from fossil fuel industries on top of her other duties. 'I realised I had the power to make changes as Director of Operations, including changing our energy contracts', Murphy explains.[20]

In April of 2021 the gallery appointed Murphy as Global Head of Environmental Sustainability. 'What's important to know about Hauser & Wirth is that environmental awareness and biodiversity protection have always been topics close to the hearts of gallery founders Iwan and Manuela Wirth', Murphy says. She continues:

Their viewpoint on the climate crisis has been shaped by conversations with artists from Camille Henrot to Rashid Johnson and Pipilotti Rist who are taking action themselves. Iwan's introduction to Haley Mellin and Art into Acres in 2021 was auspicious and has evolved into a long-term partnership resulting in permanent land conservation in Northern Guatemala, one of the most carbon dense areas on the planet. Following this introduction to Haley, we decided to move into more global initiatives which are proportional with the gallery's impact.

The creation of Murphy's role amplified Hauser & Wirth's global commitment to climate action. In addition to being a member of GCC and a founding member of Murmur (a charity formed in March 2024 to support climate action in the art and music industries), the gallery has made donations to Art into Acres and taken several steps to develop best practices and act as a model for other organisations. Among the noteworthy improvements it has achieved is the reduction of its shipping emissions by 35 per cent since 2019, mainly by shipping art via sea freight whenever possible. Murphy's paper 'Sea Freight: Unlocking the Potential for International Art Transportation' details how this was achieved, and is available on the Hauser & Wirth and GCC websites as a guide to others in the industry looking for alternatives to air freight.[21] As another example, in 2024 the gallery's West Hollywood location became the first and only commercial gallery on the West Coast of the US to achieve Leadership in Energy and Environmental Design (LEED) certification, earning LEED Platinum status through credits that address carbon, energy, water, waste, transportation, materials, health and indoor environmental quality.

Hauser & Wirth has also completed several CIRs, including a report for GRUPPENAUSSTELLUNG (June 2023 to January 2024), a group show at Hauser & Wirth Somerset, the gallery's outpost in the countryside west of London. 'What excites me about this work is that our evolution and understanding of sustainability in action is becoming embedded in our local gallery operations', says Murphy.[22] The gallery's registrars looked at CIRs from previous exhibitions at the Somerset location, some as early as Gustav Metzger's 2021 exhibition, and used this information to understand what the carbon footprint of certain decisions ranging from shipping to exhibition design would be. 'On an individual level, this was an exciting moment to illustrate how each person's role within the gallery affects the climate impact of a show and where they have agency to make change', Murphy adds.

Included in the takeaways from the *GRUPPENAUSSTELLUNG* report are the benefits of longer exhibition runs in reducing shipping, packing and material use; the need for alternatives to acrylic paint; the impact of neon lights versus LED faux neon for works that require neon (they discovered that the traditional neon had a lower impact); and the benefits of designing an exhibition with disassembly in mind so as to keep materials and furniture from ending up in landfill. One artist in the show, Mika Rottenberg, created most of her work on site, thus reducing shipping. The findings from the exhibition will inform future shows, as well as the operations of the gallery's locations globally. Such reports also help understand what areas would benefit from research and emissions reduction, including exploring additional clean energy programmes (over 70 per cent of the gallery's energy globally is from renewable sources). As with other CIRs, these findings are publicly available on Artists Commit's website. Hauser & Wirth also shares its detailed sustainability plan on the gallery's website.[23]

While these are examples of major overhauls and commitments to climate action, even actions that seem small can have a large impact. Simply using one's platform (social media, newsletters, publications etc.) to amplify climate science and educate the public are easy acts that require minimal resources. Institutions can also help the climate movement by hosting events, such as panels and programming. James Cohan and Marianne Boesky Gallery (both in New York) are among the commercial organisations where workers have taken pledges with Galleries Commit and both have offered their spaces to the group free of charge. Both galleries have also staged climate-conscious exhibitions, including Yinka Shonibare's solo show *Earth Kids* (December 2020 to January

2021) at James Cohan, for which the gallery calculated its carbon footprint and subsequently made a donation to Art into Acres. Likewise, Marianne Boesky Gallery organised *A Romance of Paradise* (March to April 2021), a solo show of works by Allison Janae Hamilton, for which they conducted Artist Commit's first ever CIR, which also marked the gallery's first carbon-conscious exhibition. The gallery donated US$35 for each work in the show (sold or unsold) to Art into Acres and continues to do so as part of its normal sales protocol. Though seemingly small steps, these exhibitions, free platforms for advocacy and donations help make climate action an everyday, system-wide part of the art industry.

Charitable Donations

Indeed, many climate pledges and plans involve charitable donations and ethical finance models that support climate action called Strategic Climate Funds (SCFs). As opposed to carbon offsets, SCFs are not understood as 'cancelling out' the carbon emissions of an organisation and shouldn't contribute to avoidance of decarbonisation. Simply put, offsetting carbon means supporting activities that reduce or store emissions to 'neutralise' one's own emissions. There are many credible organisations and initiatives that can be supported as a carbon offset. However, there is wide debate as to whether carbon offsetting can be considered a sustainable or environmentally beneficial solution. Carbon offsets can give the impression that something isn't negatively impacting the environment and so mislead consumers. They can also contribute to greenwashing (falsely posing as environmentally friendly) and can be viewed as a way to excuse unnecessary carbon emission instead of making changes to reduce emissions. Rather, as defined on GCC's website, SCFs should be prioritised over carbon offsets and should represent a proportion of earnings donated 'to support effective frontline environmental initiatives and Internal Investments that are guaranteed to remove greenhouse gas emissions directly from operations and supply chains within the 2030 timeline'.[24]

These donations can have a major impact. In 2022 over 40 institutions and individuals from the art world collectively donated funds to support the designation of the Chuyapi-Urusayhua Regional Conservation Area in Peru. The efforts were undertaken through Galleries Commit and Art into Acres, a non-profit that supports large-scale, permanent old-growth land conservation with monetary donations and through the sale of artworks. The roughly 200,000-acre permanently protected area is part of the last 1 per cent of remaining cloud forest in the world and provides potable water for 40,000 people.[25]

Art into Acres has been pivotal in catalysing climate action for artists, art workers and institutions, including many significant milestones covered in this book. Founded in 2017 by artist and conservationist Haley Mellin, Art into Acres is straightforward in concept, but its impact is remarkably complex and profound. The locally led land-conservation the non-profit supports is primarily comprised of areas of old growth and high biodiversity, as well as those significant to Indigenous groups. Art into Acres works with several international and national partners (NGOs, governments, community leaders) to carry out due diligence and establish protection for the land they conserve, including creating new National Parks, Regional Parks and Indigenous Protected Areas. Several artists and institutions have donated artworks and funds to Art into Acres, from small New York galleries like Charles Moffett to major institutions like the Metropolitan Museum of Art. 'I'm amazed by the large-scale land conservation supported by artists and institutions through Art into Acres', says Mellin. 'The support is at tens of millions of acres, at present. Larger than I'll ever be able to walk in a lifetime, and yet it was done acre by acre, artwork by artwork. One step at a time.'[26]

Similar initiatives include the environmental charity Platform Earth, which was founded in the UK in 2018 and brings together artists and scientists to support ocean health and fundraise for marine carbon-capture projects through the sales of donated works by artists such as Antony Gormley, Marina Abramović and Tracey Emin. Platform Earth's support of the Sussex Kelp Restoration Project helped ban damaging trawl-fishing in the area and has seen significant kelp forest regrowth.[27] Also leveraging the power of art for the good of the environment is Parley for the Oceans, a non-profit and global network founded by Cyrill Gutsch and Lea Stepken in 2012 after a chance encounter with Captain Paul Watson, a conservationist and activist from Sea Shepherd Conservation Society, established in Vancouver in the 1970s and now based in the US. After this meeting, Gutsch turned his design firm into an environmental organisation. Parley has partnered with several brands and arts institutions, such as Adidas and Art Basel, to raise funds and awareness of ocean health, commissioning works by over 20 artists, including Doug Aitken, Ed Ruscha and Katharina Grosse.

Galleries and auction houses are also stepping up to host fundraisers in support of climate action. Christie's became the first major auction house to establish a sustainability plan in 2021, and partnered with GCC and international environmental charity ClientEarth on the sale of five artworks in 2021 and 2022. The partnership saw the sales of works by Cecily Brown, Antony Gormley, Rashid Johnson, Beatriz Milhazes and Xie Nanxing, raising over US$6.5 million for ClientEarth, which leverages the law to enact climate action, taking on corporations for the sake of the planet.[28] Christie's furthered its climate commitment by pledging to reduce its carbon emissions by 50 per cent by 2030 and divert 90 per cent of its waste from landfill.

Art Fairs

As outlined in Chapter 1, art fairs can be particularly challenging for participants and organisers to make sustainable decisions. Fairs, with their inherently short, temporary nature, are rife with carbon-heavy activities like shipping and the creation of waste. While critics, myself included, have been questioning and criticising the climate impact of art fairs for years, a significant shift is occurring within the fairs themselves to push for sustainability. In September 2024 GCC announced an alliance of art fairs committed to environmental responsibility, including organisations agreeing to a 50 per cent reduction in greenhouse gas emissions of their operations by 2030. Thirteen art fairs representing 40 events worldwide signed the pledge, including Art Basel, ARCO, TEFAF and Untitled Art. Such alliances, as well as individual art fairs with events across the globe, offer an opportunity to scale climate action internationally. Moreover, exhibitors who participate in fairs can advocate for green practices or choose only to work with fairs that centre sustainability. In addition to the alliance, these and other fairs collaborated with GCC on an Art Fair Toolkit for Environmental Responsibility, a thorough guide to best practices, such as waste reduction and carbon reporting, also released in September 2024.

This call for a collaborative commitment joins years of individual efforts from several art fairs. Global powerhouse Art Basel has been pushing for sustainability across its events (Basel, Hong Kong, Miami Beach and Paris), details of which are outlined in depth on its website. As mentioned, some of Art Basel's fairs take place in buildings with specific climate standards, such as the Silver LEED-certified Miami Beach Convention Center, and therefore comply with the requirements of these buildings. The fair has also undertaken further initiatives, including carbon-emission reports, waste-reduction measures and ongoing programming to promote sustainability. Art Basel reuses the walls for its events, shipping them by boat to each location. The fair is also transitioning to LED lighting and recycles aisle carpets.[29] Also a global fair, Frieze, which has events in Chicago, London, Los Angeles, New York and Seoul, has published a similar sustainability plan on its website and is taking comparable steps, including reusing materials and switching to LED lights where possible, advocating for waste reduction among its exhibitors, and showcasing environmental initiatives in its programming and events.[30]

Joining these international fairs in taking sustainable steps is the Art Dealers Association of America (ADAA), which has also been working for the last few years to centre sustainability in the practices of its annual fair in New York, The Art Show. As a fair without major corporate sponsors, unlike Art Basel and Frieze which both have several, the ADAA's allocation of funds to environmental issues is a significant example of a concerted and substantial climate action. In 2022 ADAA commissioned a Sustainability Roadmap to assess the impact of The Art Show, identify short- and long-term goals and work to implement changes for green operations. The roadmap was created with architecture firm Gensler and the fair's partners: the non-profit social-service agency Henry Street Settlement, insurance company AXA XL, and Sanford L. Smith + Associates (event producers of the fair). In developing the roadmap, the ADAA used Artists Commit's Climate Impact Report model to have a select group of exhibitors track the climate impact of their activities associated with the fair. The reports, undertaken in consultation with Laura Lupton, were repeated in 2023, with all exhibitors invited to participate. Out of the 78 exhibitors at the fair, 33 submitted baseline reports, 12 submitted emissions data and 6 completed reports with extended worker and community engagement questions. These reports informed the Sustainability Roadmap and are the first of their kind to include exhibitor participation in analysing an art fair, a crucial resource to move forward sustainably and holistically as an industry and better survey the impact of its activities. Indeed, the goal of the Sustainability Roadmap is not only to improve The Art Show, but also to act as a model for all art fairs worldwide.[31]

The CIR of the 2023 Art Show highlights several interesting statistics regarding exhibitors' existing engagement with sustainable practices in general and provides insight into their operations in relation to the fair. For example, the report states that for 62 per cent of the galleries creating CIRs, it was their first ever climate action. The report also includes information on how exhibitors' employees travelled to and from the fair, such as using public transportation and walking when possible as opposed to travelling by car, an area in which all such events can work to encourage best practice. The report also showed that 85 per cent of the galleries had never calculated carbon emissions, and only one gallery reported having an existing climate-action policy. These statistics alone point to how crucial reports are for the exhibitors and for the industry at large. It also shows how much farther organisations can take their actions with the aid of a consultant.

'As The Art Show is a member-based fair and does not have corporate backing, nor operates as part of a larger corporate system, outside experts and consultants are vital to the work that we do, especially with regard to our Sustainability Roadmap Initiative', says Maureen Bray, who was Executive Director of ADAA during the inauguration of the roadmap project. 'As we progress in executing our short, mid- and long-term goals, Laura Lupton continues to help guide us as we address some of the challenges that arise along the way.'[32]

As individuals and institutions navigate their path to greener operations and implement climate actions, coaches and consultants have become increasingly useful. 'My north star in developing climate action programmes has always been overcoming the blocks to climate action that workers on the ground feel most acutely', says Lupton. 'The first block to integrating climate-responsible decisions I felt as a worker was not believing that my personal values were appropriate to impose at work. This is partially why so much of our work now emphasizes supporting workers.'[33] Indeed, galleries and institutions across the industry are increasingly including diversity, equity and inclusion in their sustainability pledges and climate-action plans, an important recognition of the intersectionality of social and climate justices.

Funding

To hire such consultants, of course, requires funds, which, as outlined in Chapter 1, remains a significant issue across the art industry. Thankfully, there are several grant-giving organisations that have made significant strides to support climate-related projects, such as Creative Time, which funds and commissions public art worldwide, including several initiatives related to sustainability, in line with its emphasis on championing artworks that respond to urgent issues. The Mellon Foundation also supports charities in the US – and outside the US with 501(c)(3) equivalency – on projects related to climate change and artistic approaches to environmentalism, among other non-art related areas, including education and public knowledge. Among the grants the Mellon Foundation offers is its Presidential Initiatives scheme, which recognises the importance of art and humanities in addressing critical issues, including climate change. In the UK, the London Museum offers climate-action grants for accredited London museums to support environmental responsibility. Taking a more global perspective, the British Council awards cultural institutions and artists in South Asia with grants of £15,000 for sustainable practices and artistic projects responding to climate change.

Recognising the importance of funding environmental initiatives, organisations are increasingly creating climate-specific grants, such as those supported by Teiger Foundation. Established in 2008 by the late collector and museum patron David Teiger, the foundation supports US-based curatorial initiatives with a range of grants with funding up to US$150,000 depending on the type of project. Considering specific areas within the art industry in need of support, Teiger Foundation understood the importance of climate action. 'Out of the urgent issues we're facing, climate change is perhaps the most urgent', says Larissa Harris, Executive Director of Teiger Foundation. 'The question isn't why we decided to fund climate action, but rather why others are not. I truly believe anyone with access to funds should be devoting some of those funds to climate action.'[34]

In 2021 Teiger Foundation began conversations with members of Partners for Arts Climate Targets (PACT), a coalition to catalyse climate action as discussed later in this chapter. Harris had been actively engaging with grassroots climate groups that formed during the COVID-19 pandemic and wanted to understand how the foundation could foster engagement with climate action. 'The work groups like GCC, Art into Acres, and Artists Commit were doing, and still are doing, was remarkably innovative and sensitive to the intersectional nature of climate justice, taking into account things like worker capacity', says Harris. To this end, the foundation directly supported Artists Commit, Art + Climate Action, GCC, Ki Culture and Art into Acres in 2022 and 2023.

Through its conversations with these groups, as well as curators in the field, Teiger Foundation took its support of climate action further with a climate-specific grant, which began in a pilot phase in 2023. For the pilot programme, the foundation selected six of its curatorial grantees and paired them for a year with a sustainability coach, Alexa Steiner of Rute Collaborative, to develop a tailored climate plan, allocating additional funding of up to US$20,000 to execute that plan. In September 2024 Teiger Foundation took its findings from the pilot programme and officially launched Climate Action for Curators, which grant applicants can opt into in addition to their curatorial grants. The inaugural programme awarded five grantees with additional funds of up to US$25,000 to implement the plan devised alongside their sustainability coach.

Like the collaboration between the ADAA, consultant Laura Lupton and Gensler, the coaching Teiger Foundation provides with Alexa Steiner is crucial for its grantees, as Harris explains:

> The Climate Action for Curators grantees are so motivated and eager to take action, but they don't always have the tools or time to make a plan – not to mention that non-profits are historically underfunded. I realized we couldn't just give money, because people weren't yet equipped to know what to do with that money, and we couldn't just give a coach, because people need funds to enact their plans. We want to support people in a way that is sustainable and empowering, and that requires both coaching and funding.

For the pilot programme, grantees met with Steiner at least monthly, continually workshopping issues and devising tailored plans. The ongoing feedback helped to implement and rework changes in real time and ensure their ongoing sustainability. These plans have been crucial for the grantees to identify their specific needs. 'One of the things we learned in this process is how dissimilar people's experiences will be in creating a climate plan', says grantee Andrea Andersson, Founding Director and Chief Curator of Rivers Institute for Contemporary Art & Thought. 'The support we had through Alexa's coaching and the knowledge-sharing Rute Collaborative brought in from other grant-ees was integral to us taking action.'[35] The New Orleans-based art and research non-profit stages exhibitions all over the country in long-form partnerships with other institutions, including a series of shows and publications that highlight the ways Rivers Institute conducts research and provides a platform for art and artists of the global diaspora, which earned the institute the Teiger grant.

Through the climate-action pilot programme, Rivers developed a plan to rethink systems and protocols throughout its operations, tools it can bring to the institutions it partners with. Rivers is also seeking to transition its energy from the grid, thus becoming climate resilient in the face of increasingly devastating storms and the power-outages that come with them, a common occurrence in New Orleans. 'We don't have the time or resources to become students of the science and systems involved with going off-grid', Andersson says. 'Teiger became the engine that fueled our process. We looked at every decision we normally make and asked, "Can this be done differently?"' As an example, for a recent exhibition, the team began planning the deinstallation process two months before the show ended and was able to find a new home for every purpose-built element, such as vitrines and plinths, by reaching out to its local network of artists and collectives. 'It took time and advance planning, but this is the kind of thinking we need to do to ensure that materials don't end up in landfills', Andersson explains. 'Now that this system is in place, we can replicate the process going forward.'

Also a Teiger pilot-programme participant, Alex Klein, Head Curator and Director of Curatorial Affairs at The Contemporary Austin, applied for the Teiger curatorial grant for *Nature Never Loses*, a 2024 survey show of work by Carl Cheng, an interdisciplinary, experimental artist who works at the overlap of identity, ecology and technology. 'The climate action programme allowed us to try to embody the ecological principles of Carl's practice in the way we staged the show', says Klein.[36] As *Nature Never Loses* will travel to several locations worldwide until early 2027, the exhibition presents a unique opportunity to track the climate impact over the next few years, a period likely to see developments as the industry responds to climate change.

'The work with Rute will help us understand what it looks like to resource-share between multiple organizations while always keeping sustainable materials and processes in mind', says Klein. For example, the museum now has a sustainability clause in its agreements for artists and partnering institutions that outlines the steps it is taking to make climate-conscious decisions and includes resources on how others can do the same, an important move in encouraging sustainable operations across the industry.

While Teiger Foundation supports climate action at a curatorial level, the Frankenthaler Climate Initiative (FCI) aims to catalyse climate action within an institution's infrastructure. The FCI was established in 2021 as the United States's first nationwide grant-making programme to support clean-energy usage and energy efficiency for institutions in the visual arts. Developed in collaboration with the Helen Frankenthaler Foundation, Environment & Culture Partners and sustainability thinktank RMI, the FCI brings together each group's skills, with the Helen Frankenthaler Foundation leveraging its legacy as an established grant-giving non-profit, RMI bringing in technical expertise in clean-energy systems, and Environment & Culture Partners demystifying the complex facets of climate action and sustainability for the arts and culture sectors. 'What excites me about climate action is that it is collaborative and will take working together to make a difference', says James Merle Thomas, Deputy Director of the Helen Frankenthaler Foundation. 'These conversations cannot exist in vacuums.'[37]

Together the team developed the FCI grant programme, focusing on energy – one of the major issues facing the industry, both in terms of the ageing or outdated infrastructures of many institutions, as well as the stringent standards for climate control discussed in Chapter 1. The grant aims to help institutions adapt for climate resiliency and miti-gate the impact of their operations on the environment. Assessing and managing the energy consumption of buildings is crucial not only to achieve climate-conscious operations, but also to reduce the financial burden of energy bills. 'We see major museums spending as much as 30 per cent of their budget on energy', says Thomas. The upfront costs of things like improved HVAC systems can be prohibitive, but these changes show long-term financial benefits.

Since its launch in 2021, the FCI grant has distributed over US$14 million to over 200 organisations in the visual arts in the US, with the goal of dispersing US$15 million total over five years. The grants span a wide range both in size and in the scale and complexity of the project being supported, which often reflects where the grantee is on their climate-action and sustainability journey, thus providing a greater diversity of entry points for applicants. At the lower end, the Catalyst Grants provide funds of up to US$15,000 and support small spaces, first climate actions or stand-alone projects with short turnarounds, while the higher end encourages institutions to undertake innovative, major infrastructural changes with grants of up to US$100,000. The projects the FCI supports help institutions assess their environmental impact, and form and implement plans to mitigate this, while also promoting clean energy. Grantees include major museums, art schools, non-profits and community art centres, among other visual-arts organisations. As part of the initiative, FCI grantees track and report their energy usage and greenhouse gas emissions with Energy Star® Portfolio Manager®. These reports are useful tools for grantees to understand their own climate impact. Additionally, some energy-related grants require information on the institution's current emissions and energy usage, so tracking this data prepares them for future proposals. Organisations can also use their reports to advocate for funding from donors when such changes are proven to reduce costs over time. Such reports are helpful to establish a survey of energy consumption in the visual arts in general, offering other institutions a baseline with which to compare their own operations.

Aligning Efforts

Many climate groups have cited information-sharing as one of their founding principles. In 2023 the Network of European Museum Organisations (NEMO) created a map on its website that tracks how museums are responding to the climate crisis, helping to keep this information organised and readily available for others to learn from.[38] The crowdsourced initiative features projects of all sizes, including exhibition listings, plans for improved operations, and announcements of resources and programmes. Galleries Commit has a similar resource called the Climate Action Database where users can share resources and information on projects they've undertaken, including climate-action plans. The Climate Action Database is also hosted on the websites of Artists Commit and Art + Climate Action, a group founded in 2020 to align Bay Area artists, art workers and institutions on issues of climate change. The New York and Amsterdam-based non-profit Art Switch (formerly Art/Switch) also unites climate-conscious professionals in the art world and hosts online conferences that bring together international specialists and experts to discuss a range of topics, including sustainable exhibitions and rethinking the logistics of transportation and climate control.

Museum groups have also formed industry-wide networks to improve practices and share resources, including the UK Museum Association's Museum for Climate Justice, the ICOM Sustainability Working Group, and the American Association of Museums Environment and Climate Network. On the gallery front, Galleries Commit aligned with Art to Zero, Art + Climate Action and GCC's Los Angeles branch to launch Climate Action 8 x 8 in 2022. The initiative outlines eight climate actions centred around eight areas of operations, including measuring and mitigating carbon emissions, green packaging and shipping solutions, supporting workers and reducing waste. Galleries that undertake this initiative and complete a report can become part of Climate Action 8 x 8. In 2023 GCC launched a similar programme called Active Membership to acknowledge members who have completed a carbon audit or emissions report within the last two years, have established and maintained a green team, and have included a statement of their commitment to environmental responsibility on their website. Members who do so receive a badge that can be used for communications and on their websites, and Active Membership is reevaluated annually. These advanced commitments illustrate how climate groups can hold members accountable to take action and help to fight against greenwashing, since simply taking a pledge does not ensure action.

In another effort to unify climate action, in the summer of 2021 seven groups (Art into Acres, Art + Climate Action, Art Switch, Art to Zero, GCC, Galleries Commit and Ki Culture) formed Partners for Arts Climate Targets (PACT), a coalition to catalyse climate action and align the art industry with the Paris Agreement. International in scope and contributing different skills and expertise thanks to the diverse backgrounds of the founding members, the group, which was joined by Artists Commit shortly after its founding, is centred on four pillars: reducing emissions, transitioning to zero waste, creating unified standards and implementing intersectional environmentalism that acknowledges the overlap of environmental and social justice.[39]

A similar collaborative initiative was launched in September 2023 called Art Charter for Climate Action (ACCA). Created by the International Committee for Museums and Collections of Modern Art (CIMAM), GCC, Julie's Bicycle and ART 2030, the charter also aims to align the global art industry with the Paris Agreement, uniting the industry with a framework to: 'implement environmental values as central to sector practices; reduce the negative environmental impact of developing, producing, transporting, and exhibiting visual art; support adaptation and future resilience of the sector; and contribute to developing a green and environmentally just future'.[40] ACCA brings together over 1000 members from more than 70 countries, representing a wide range of professionals and institutions across the art world. In April 2024, at the Venice Biennale, the ACCA Founding Alliance (the organisations that created the charter) announced its official partnership with the UN's environmental branch, the United Nations Framework Convention on Climate Change, with ACCA becoming the visual-arts pillar of the UN Climate Change's Entertainment & Culture for Climate Action alliance. The partnership demonstrates the UN's recognition of the importance of art in fighting climate change.

All of these efforts to align climate action are significant and, in many ways, a defining characteristic of what climate action in the art world looks like today. We are seeing the results of years of work to identify the issues, find solutions, share results and take action together for industry-wide change. We are finally establishing examples of climate-conscious operations and understanding what it will take to approach a greener future for the art world. The question now is: what's next?

4

What's Next? The Future of Climate Action in the Art World

When I began this book in February 2024, I felt confident that I could predict the general appearance of the future of climate action in the art world, at least for the near future. The years since the pandemic have seen great momentum and enthusiasm to align efforts, support one another and scale climate action to the global scale of the art industry. That said, we are only in the first phase of concerted efforts to catalyse climate action and make the industry sustainable. There are many urgent issues still facing the art world. For some, efforts are underway to improve these areas. By the time this book is published, I'm sure more answers will have emerged.

Predicting the future is futile, if not naive, but moments of self-reflection are crucial. The enthusiasm for climate action that marked the last few years still exists, but the efforts undertaken are far too young to fully understand their impact. We don't know which individuals and communities are falling through the cracks. We are only beginning to address issues, create reports, establish baselines and improve systems. Steps forward are being made, and steps back might also be necessary. This will be true forever as the industry continues to establish best practices in response to the changing climate.

Ongoing Issues

Funding remains a major issue in developing, implementing and sustaining climate-action plans. Grants can offer temporary relief, but ongoing support is necessary to continue to improve climate-conscious decisions. There are many ways individuals and institutions garner funds, from museum boards and donors to grants and collectors. The reports and research being done to show the importance of climate action (especially the research that illustrates the financial benefit of such action) are crucial in making an argument for further greening of the art industry. On a micro level, an individual collector can decide to support an artist or gallery that centres climate action. On a macro level, museum boards can allocate funds for clean energy, climate-related exhibitions and programmes, and acquisitions of artworks by artists engaging with the environment.

Logistics and supporting industries also need to be improved, particularly shipping. 'The more research we do individually and as an industry, the more we can understand the bigger picture of shipping', says Cliodhna Murphy of Hauser & Wirth. 'Currently, shipping agents are more familiar with air and road transportation as opposed to sea freight. There's a lot of education that needs to happen within the art industry to ask better questions of shippers and give them the confidence to offer low-carbon alternatives. The more we ask, the greater chance things will change.'[1]

Packing materials are also an area ripe for exploration. Studies are underway, but we need more to broaden the scope and scale of this work. Moreover, further analysis needs to be done to think beyond just the carbon footprint when analysing the climate impact of materials, which should also take into consideration things like their toxicity.

The more we learn about sustainability, the more complicated the conversation becomes. Guidelines are constantly being updated as new reports emerge. Navigating this information will remain an ongoing roadblock for individuals and institutions with limited time, resources, funds and expertise. Information-sharing must continue, and research and reporting need to be supported. In-house sustainability roles should be created where possible, and funds devoted to climate action have to become part of strategic planning.

All organisations in the art world with physical spaces face the same issues that impact the built environment: infrastructures age and adaptation is costly or impossible. The fact is that climate change has shifted the viability of many infrastructures. Institutions are tackling this on individual levels, often in response to climate disasters, but it's an issue that also needs to be addressed collectively. In an opinion piece for CNN, the climate writer Jeff Goodell underscored this fact more broadly: 'We have built our world for a climate that no longer exists'.[2] Year after year, we are seeing this unfold in museums and cultural heritage sites across the globe. In the UK, in 2022, a summer heatwave forced museums, including the British Museum and the Victoria & Albert Museum, to temporarily close some galleries and even entire buildings. The Acropolis in Greece is now accustomed to such interruptions, closing in 2023 and again in 2024 due to excess heat with temperatures reaching 107 degrees Fahrenheit. The site has also had to close due to wildfires. What climate change means for such cultural heritage sites where adapting infrastructures isn't possible remains to be seen.

This is as true for daily operations in the face of a climate that is breaking down as it is for institutions' resiliency against disasters. Take, for example, Tate Britain in London. In 1928 the River Thames broke its banks, killing 14 people and leaving thousands without homes. The flood also entered what was then the Tate Gallery, filling the lower-level galleries and basement, destroying 18 works and damaging nearly 300 others. Efforts to prevent against such inundation in the museum now exist, but London, like much of the world, continues to face rising waters and threats of floods.[3] The infrastructure in place to protect against flooding, such as the Thames Barrier, which was completed in 1982 and protects much of the Greater London floodplain, was constructed based on earlier sea-level models. Climate change has shifted these models and sea levels have risen rapidly, meaning many of the city's defences will have to be refortified or reconstructed years sooner than expected.[4] Tate Britain adapted in the past, and it may need to do so again – before rather than after a future climate emergency.

As climate change worsens, so too do the climate events we face and all institutions, regardless of the age or condition of their infrastructures, must work to deal with them. While issues like floods were once only concerns for low-lying and coastal communities, the effects of climate change are taking a toll in areas where they previously were rarely seen. In August 2023 the California African American Museum in Los Angeles experienced flood damage as a result of the unprecedented rain brought by Tropical Storm Hilary. The museum's building, which was constructed in the 1980s, was forced to close for repairs and didn't reopen for nearly nine months. Some institutions are working to adapt their infrastructures and grounds to be resilient as climate change worsens, but many others are forced to take a reactive approach.

In addressing the impact of climate change, it's important to recognise that not all communities face the same consequences. Studies have shown that climate change disproportionately affects marginalised communities worldwide.[5] In the US communities of colour in particular face increased health risks.[6] This disproportionate impact extends to the art world. In December 2023 the Association of African American Museums (AAAM) circulated a press release declaring the heightened effects of climate change on Black museums and cultural institutions. Included in AAAM's statement was a call to action for its members to work alongside local communities, policymakers and stakeholders to advocate for policies and strategic planning that support these historic cultural centres that are at risk.[7] Often built in coastal zones on or near historic sites where enslaved Africans were brought to the US, these institutions face a greater threat of floods and storm damage due to older infrastructures and fewer resources.[8] We must address this inequity to move forward as a sustainable, resilient industry for all.

Beyond surviving climate change, buildings need to have better energy systems and organisations need to transition to clean energy.

'When evaluating progress in climate-action commitments by the various sectors of the art world, it is clear that accessible entry-points such as shifting to renewable energy or reducing travel haven't been engaged by most; this needs to change, and it needs to change now', says Haley Mellin.[9] Grants like the FCI are crucial in supporting such endeavours, but there are many infrastructures in need of large-scale improvements. Along the same lines, while there are signs that this is underway, the industry needs to reevaluate the strict climate-control standards that consume unnecessary energy and produce added waste. This includes further studies on climate-control regulations to loosen the narrow requirements and make them more adaptable. This also means working with partnering institutions on flexible loan agreements.

Audience Activities

There are many questions that remain in understanding the art world's impact on the climate. How far does its responsibility extend and where does that of the audience begin? Can the industry take into account the actions of visitors travelling to art shows and events, or collectors buying artwork? While an artist or dealer might decide only to sell to local collectors, they can't control what that collector does with the work once it is purchased. The painting might live alone in a giant, energy-draining storage facility or it might fly across the world to the buyer's multiple homes. Museums can encourage visitors to use public transportation or fossil fuel-free methods of travel, and can even incentivise such actions with schemes like free or reduced admission, but they can't force the public to act a certain way. Art fairs can ask exhibitors to report their methods of transporting both people and artworks, and require that specific means be considered first, but these events rely upon visitors from all corners of the world to attend. Efforts to account for these factors are being made, such as the ADAA Art Show's climate-impact report tracking exhibitor travel, but this is ultimately a nascent area of investigation in the industry.

Conclusion: Climate Action in the Future

With all of the work achieved since 2020, we are already seeing signs that a new chapter is emerging in climate action in the art world. The first phase, generally speaking, saw the industry acknowledge its responsibility to be environmentally sustainable, take pledges to understanding its impact and identify areas of improvement, and launch efforts to implement best practices. We are slowly beginning to understand what these efforts and actions have meant for the sector and what practices best serve a green future.

If the last few years have taught us anything, it's that in the fight against the climate crisis, adaptation is key. GCC's announcement in September 2024 that it would close all international branches outside of London was surprising, but it also offers an important lesson in self-reflection. GCC felt there was a better path forward to grow and support the art industry and use the resources available to them in a way that is responsible and sustainable. Since launching in 2020, its membership has steadily increased and enthusiasm for the services the charity can provide has clearly had a significant impact, but GCC, like other climate initiatives, is still young and still understanding how to grow sustainably. Moreover, as with virtually all non-profits in the sector, it needs funding. For now, GCC plans to maintain its global network and take feedback it has received from its members and international branches to better support them through an advocacy and empowerment programme.[10]

Sometimes difficult decisions are necessary to succeed in the long run but, across the board, these decisions need to continue to be made. At every level, green plans must be evaluated regularly and, if needed, revised. There are challenges inherent in this, namely that an evolving framework requires a continuous flow of resources to fund the staff responsible for development. We need more research, data and reporting to set benchmarks and analyse the work underway, better understand how to move forward, and empower individuals and institutions to tackle the issues with knowledge and confidence. As new challenges in the climate crisis emerge, new solutions will need to be developed and the same roadblocks that faced the initial climate plans will arise all over again.

Perhaps the most pressing issue facing the art world is the fact that sustainability and climate action still are not widely understood as 'a thing'. We need to make them a thing. The intersection of art and climate action cannot exist in a silo. These conversations have to spread, and more voices must be welcomed and heard. Sustainability policies must be written into the governing documents and operations of institutions, from job descriptions to contracts with vendors and partners.

My hope for the future of climate action in the art world is that climate-conscious decisions become the first decisions. The industry must centre environmental sustainability, support green practices and ban wasteful ones. What this looks like, I can't say for sure. Perhaps it's a regulatory board and the corporatisation of climate action. Perhaps it's imposing fines or taxes. Perhaps it lies in the grassroots initiatives galvanising others to take action. For now, we must enact the climate pledges so many in the art world have made. We must support best practices and hold each other accountable. Above all, we must scale the existing efforts to the global scale of the industry. The benchmark year of 2030 is fast approaching, and if the art world is going to meet the standards of the Paris Accord, we had better get to work.

Notes

Introduction

1 'Secretary-General's Message on the Hottest Summer on Record', United Nations press release, 6 September 2024.
2 'About', Culture Declares Emergency website, n.d., https://www.culturedeclares.org/about/.

1: Identifying the Issues

1 In 2021 Julie's Bicycle used case studies of artist studios, museums, auction houses, shippers and art fairs and estimated that the carbon footprint of the global visual arts sector was 70 million metric tons CO_2 equivalent, more than many countries, including Peru and Greece. 'Art to Zero', Julie's Bicycle, 10 May 2021, https://juliesbicycle.com/resource/the-art-of-zero/.
2 As well as to 'periodically assess the collective progress towards achieving the purpose of this agreement and its long-term goals; and provide financing to developing countries to mitigate climate change, strengthen resilience and enhance abilities to adapt to climate impacts'. 'The Paris Agreement', United Nations, n.d., https://www.un.org/en/climatechange/paris-agreement.
3 For an in-depth analysis of the term net zero and its nuances and pitfalls, see Sam Fankhauser et al., 'The Meaning of Net Zero and How to Get it Right',

Nature Climate Change, 2022, https://doi.org/10.1038/s41558-021-01245-w.

4 'For a Livable Climate: Net-zero Commitments Must Be Backed by Credible Action', United Nations website, n.d., https://www.un.org/en/climatechange/net-zero-coalition.

5 'The Paris Agreement', United Nations Climate Change, n.d., https://unfccc.int/process-and-meetings/the-paris-agreement.

6 'FAQ', Greenhouse Gas Protocol's website, n.d., https://ghgprotocol.org/sites/default/files/standards_supporting/FAQ.pdf.

7 For a detailed explanation of carbon footprint scopes 1, 2 and 3, and net zero, see Julie's Bicycle's 'Spotlight Programme: Transitioning to Net Zero', n.d., https://juliesbicycle.com/wp-content/uploads/2022/04/JB112-New-Zero-Spotlight-V10.pdf.

8 Author interview with Heath Lowndes of GCC, August 2024. When discussing non-UK GCC branches in this book, I refer to them in the present tense because some are still in existence despite no longer officially being under the umbrella of GCC.

9 Alex Marshall, 'As Energy Costs Bite, Museums Rethink a Conservation Credo', *The New York Times*, 1 February 2023, https://www.nytimes.com/2023/02/01/arts/design/museums-energy-climate-control.html.

10 ibid.

11 ibid.

12 Caitlin Southwick, 'Collections Management and Conservation', in Nick Merriman (ed.), *Museums and the Climate Crisis*, Abingdon, 2024, p.125.

13 Maria Balshaw, 'The 100 Year Future: Museums and the Climate and Nature Crisis', in ibid., p.150.

14 'The Climate Benefit of Ocean vs Air Transport of Artworks', Gallery Climate Coalition, n.d., https://galleryclimatecoalition.org/usr/library/documents/main/the-climate-benefits-of-ocean-vs-air-transport-of-artworks.pdf.

15 Maria Balshaw, op.cit., p.151.

16 'Sustainability', Christie's, n.d., https://www.christies.com/services/sustainability/overview.

17 'Shipper Sustainable Services Survey', Gallery Climate Coalition, n.d., https://galleryclimatecoalition.org/ssc/shipper-survey/.

18 For a thorough overview of packing materials, waste and recycling, see the e-book 'Waste & Materials Ki Book' by Kim Kraczon, Director of Materials

at Ki Culture, n.d., https://www.kiculture.org/ki-books/. Also see 'Packaging', Gallery Climate Coalition, n.d., https://galleryclimatecoalition.org/packaging/.

19 Author interviews with Cliodhna Murphy of Hauser & Wirth, July 2024, and Heath Lowndes of GCC, August 2024.

20 Annabel Keenan, 'The Environmental Toll of the Art World: How Are Fairs Contending with Miami's Fragile Environment?', *The Art Newspaper*, 28 November 2022, https://www.theartnewspaper.com/2022/11/28/the-environmental-toll-of-the-art-world-how-are-fairs-contending-with-miamis-fragile-environment.

21 Joe Ware, 'Fairs Are One of the Art World's Biggest Sources of Emissions, so How Can They Become More Green?', *The Art Newspaper*, 11 October 2024, https://www.theartnewspaper.com/2024/10/11/fairs-are-on-the-art-worlds-biggest-sources-of-emissionshow-can-they-become-more-green.

22 'Sustainable Shipper Services Survey 2023', Gallery Climate Coalition, n.d., https://galleryclimatecoalition.org/usr/library/documents/main/_gcc_shipper-survey-results_23.pdf.

23 'Art Basel Successfully Concludes its 2024 Edition under the Leadership of New Show Director Maike Cruse', Art Basel press release, 16 June 2024, https://www.artbasel.com/stories/art-basel-successfully-concludes-its-2024-edition-under-the-leadership-of-new-show-director-maike-cruse.

24 'Sustainability', Art Basel, n.d., https://www.artbasel.com/sustainability. Information confirmed by Art Basel spokesperson via email on 2 November 2024.

25 Jamie Beevor et al., 'Jetting Away with it', Possible, July 2023, https://docs.google.com/document/d/1WdGEPGb7W5QvomzJCmtSDwG_NdvtcU3zxzpQNIZ-mH0/edit#heading=h.u6xdl3yooc6d.

26 'Ban Private Jets', Greenpeace, n.d., https://www.greenpeace.org/international/act/ban-private-jets/.

27 Louisa Buck, 'Jetting Away with it: The Challenge of Parting the Super-rich from their Private Planes', *The Art Newspaper*, 4 August 2023, https://www.theartnewspaper.com/2023/08/04/jetting-away-with-it-the-challenge-of-parting-the-super-rich-from-their-private-planes.

28 'United States May Lose One-third of All Museums, New Survey Shows', American Alliance of Museums press release, 22 July 2020, https://www.aam-us.org/2020/07/22/united-states-may-lose-one-third-of-all-museums-new-survey-shows/.

29 Douglas Worts, 'Museums as Catalysts of Cultural Adaptation: the "Inside-Outside Model"', in Nick Merriman, op.cit., p.69.

2: Art and Artists Become Catalysts for Change

1   Jeffrey Kastner and Brian Wallis (eds), *Land and Environment Art*, London, 1998, p.12.
2   'Detroit Metro Area Ranks 13th Worst in Nation for Annual Particle Pollution, According to the 2024 "State of the Air" Report', American Lung Association press release, 24 April 2024, https://www.lung.org/media/press-releases/detroit-sota-fy23.
3   Sarah Cwiek, 'Detroit Stellantis Plant Hit with Fine for Eighth Environmental Violation', *Michigan Public*, 18 June 2023, https://www.michiganpublic.org/environment-climate-change/2023-06-18/detroit-stellantis-plant-hit-with-fine-for-eighth-environmental-violation.
4   Annabel Keenan, '"Iron Fist in a Velvet Glove": Detroit Public Sculpture Tracks Air Quality and Cleans the Polluted Environment', *The Art Newspaper*, 3 June 2024, https://www.theartnewspaper.com/2024/06/03/jordan-weber-detroit-public-sculpture-air-quality-environmental-racism.
5   'Air Quality and Climate Change Research', United States Environmental Protection Agency, 5 February 2024, https://www.epa.gov/air-research/air-quality-and-climate-change-research.
6   Annabel Keenan, 'What Would Inspire Climate Action? Perhaps an Orange Sky', *The New York Times*, 18 October 2023, https://www.nytimes.com/2023/10/18/arts/design/blanton-museum-climate-change-exhibit-orange-sky.html.
7   Jena Brooker, '"Decades of Racism": Black Detroiters Face Foul Odor after Jeep Factory Expands', *The Guardian*, 26 June 2023, https://www.theguardian.com/us-news/2023/jun/26/east-canfield-detroit-black-community-displaced-stellantis.
8   'Detroit: The Current Status of Asthma Burden', Michigan Department of Health & Human Services, 2021.
9   'Texas: State Profile and Energy Estimates', U.S. Energy Information Administration, 18 July 2024, https://www.eia.gov/state/analysis.php?sid=TX.
10 'Olafur Eliasson and Minik Rosing *Ice Watch*', Tate, December 2018, https://www.tate.org.uk/whats-on/tate-modern/olafur-eliasson-and-minik-rosing-ice-watch.

11 'Ice Watch London', Julie's Bicycle, 8 November 2019, https://juliesbicycle. com/news-opinion/ice-watch-london-2018/.

12 'Inside the Ice: Ice Watch London, Carbon Footprint,' Julie's Bicycle, February 2019, https://olafureliasson-net.fra1.cdn.digitaloceanspaces.com/ static_press/icewatchlondon/Ice_Watch_London_Carbon_Footprint.pdf.

13 Naomi Rea, 'Olafur Eliasson Hauls 30 Icebergs to London, Inviting the Public to Contemplate the Devastating Effects of Climate Change', *Artnet News*, 11 December 2018, https://news.artnet.com/art-world/olafur-eliasson- ice-watch-london-1416811.

14 Annabel Keenan, 'Experience the World as a Spider in Tomás Saraceno's New Exhibition at The Shed', *The Art Newspaper*, 22 February 2022, https://www. theartnewspaper.com/2022/02/22/tomas-saracenos-spiders-webs-the-shed.

15 'What We Do and Why', Anti-Uranium Mapping Project, n.d., https://www. antiuraniummappingproject.com.

16 'Anonymous Was A Woman and New York Foundation for the Arts (NYFA) Announce 2024 Environmental Art Grants Recipients', NYFA press release, 20 August 2024, https://www.nyfa.org/blog/anonymous-was-a-woman-and- new-york-foundation-for-the-arts-nyfa-announce-2024-environmental-art- grants-recipients/.

17 A PDF of the essay is available on the studio's website, n.d., https://res. cloudinary.com/olafureliasson-net/image/upload/pdf/fourteen-views-of- studio-olafur-eliassons-sustainability-agenda_23868.pdf.

18 Olafur Eliasson et al., 'Fourteen Views of Studio Olafur Eliasson's Sustainability Agenda, 2020', in *Olafur Eliasson: Sometimes the river is the bridge*, Museum of Contemporary Art, Tokyo, 2020, pp 142–50.

19 Annabel Keenan, 'Launch of Artists Commit Intensifies the Push to Act on Climate Change', *The Art Newspaper*, 22 April 2021, https://www. theartnewspaper.com/2021/04/22/launch-of-artists-commit-intensifies-the- push-to-act-on-climate-change.

20 Robin F. Williams's Studio Climate Policy and CIR are available at https:// www.artistscommit.com/reports/robin-williams-ppow.

21 Matthew Conlen, 'How Much Carbon Dioxide Are We Emitting?', NASA, 15 July 2021, https://science.nasa.gov/science-research/earth-science/climate- science/how-much-carbon-dioxide-are-we-emitting/.

22 'What Is a Carbon Footprint', The Nature Conservancy, n.d., https://www. nature.org/en-us/get-involved/how-to-help/carbon-footprint-calculator.

23 Aileen Getty, 'I Fund Climate Activism – and I Applaud the Van Gogh Protest', *The Guardian*, 22 October 2022, https://www.theguardian.com/commentisfree/2022/oct/22/just-stop-oil-van-gogh-national-gallery-aileen-getty.

24 'Sustainability', Museum of Modern Art, New York, n.d., https://www.moma.org/about/sustainability/.

25 Benjamin Sutton, '"MoMA, Dump Kravis": Activists Call on Museum to Break up with Board Chair in Valentine's Day Protest', *The Art Newspaper*, 14 February 2024, https://www.theartnewspaper.com/2024/02/14/museum-modern-art-climate-protest-kravis-valentines-day.

26 Texts and conversations between the author and eye-witnesses, June and July 2024.

27 Melissa Guerrero, 'MoMA's Garden Party Honors Joan Jonas, LaToya Ruby Frazier and Refik Anadol', *The New York Times*, 5 June 2024, https://www.nytimes.com/2024/06/05/style/moma-joan-jonas-latoya-ruby-frazier.html.

28 Benjamin Sutton, '"We Charge You with Ecocide": Climate Protestors Call for Ouster of Museum of Modern Art Board Chair at Gala', *The Art Newspaper*, 7 June 2023, https://www.theartnewspaper.com/2023/06/07/climate-protest-museum-modern-art-new-york-gala-henry-kravis.

29 Benjamin Sutton, 'Climate Protestors Call for Removal of MoMA's Board Chair over Ties to Fossil Fuel Industry', *The Art Newspaper*, 15 September 2023, https://www.theartnewspaper.com/2023/09/15/museum-modern-art-protesters-climate-change-fossil-fuel-marie-josee-henry-kravis-kkr.

30 Nick Clark, 'BP to End Controversial Sponsorship of Tate in 2017', *Independent*, 11 March 2016, https://www.independent.co.uk/arts-entertainment/art/news/bp-to-end-controversial-sponsorship-of-tate-in-2017-a6923471.html.

31 'Drop the Shell', Fossil Free Culture, 30 May 2017, https://fossilfreeculture.nl/portfolio/drop-the-shell/.

32 Kathleen Massara, 'Environmental Activists Focus on Museums that Take Oil Money', *The New York Times*, 9 October 2018, https://www.nytimes.com/2018/10/09/business/environmental-activists-take-on-oil-money.html.

33 Martin Bailey, 'Shell Sponsorship Deal with Amsterdam's Van Gogh Museum Ends', *The Art Newspaper*, 29 August 2018, https://www.theartnewspaper.com/2018/08/29/shell-sponsorship-deal-with-amsterdams-van-gogh-museum-ends.

3: Climate Commitments Turn into Climate Action

1   Lupton is also a co-founder of Galleries Commit, Artists Commit, GCC New York and Barder.

2   Email to the author, 20 August 2024.

3   This and subsequent quotes, email to the author, 24 May 2024.

4   Anna Clark and Sarahbeth Maney, 'Ten Years After the Flint Water Crisis, Distrust and Anger Linger', *ProPublica*, 4 May 2024, https://www.propublica.org/article/flint-michigan-water-crisis-ten-years-after.

5   'Tate and Climate Change', Tate, n.d., https://www.tate.org.uk/about-us/tate-and-climate-change.

6   'Climate and Ecology', Horniman, January 2020, https://www.horniman.ac.uk/about-the-horniman/climate-and-ecology/.

7   Nick Merriman, op.cit., pp 7–13.

8   'Committing to a Climate-Conscious Future for NYC Galleries: Our Call to Action', Galleries Commit mission statement, https://www.galleriescommit.com.

9   Email to the author, 20 May 2024.

10 'MOCA Forms Environmental Council', MOCA press release, 14 October 2020, https://www.moca.org/storage/app/media/Press%20Releases/2020/MOCA%20FORMS%20ENVIRONMENTAL%20COUNCIL.pdf.

11 I had the opportunity to organise and moderate a panel with artists Andrea Bowers, Patty Chang, Madeline Hollander and Jonah Jacobs in August 2022. Entitled 'Approaches to Sustainability: A Conversation with Artists Engaging with Environmental Issues', the event highlighted the diversity of approaches to climate action and sustainability in the art world to inspire the audience to consider how the topics might relate to their own lives.

12 Mellin will vacate her co-chair role in 2025 to allow for new perspectives on the council. Email to the author, 18 July 2024.

13 'Pipilotti Rist: The Museum of Contemporary Art, Los Angeles', Climate Impact Report, Artists Commit, 10 October 2021, https://www.artistscommit.com/reports/pipilotti-rist-moca.

14 'Bizot's Refreshed Green Protocol 2023', Bizot, December 2023, https://www.cimam.org/sustainability-and-ecology-museum-practice/bizot-green-protocol/.

15 'Climate Neutrality 2030', Guggenheim Bilbao, n.d., https://www.guggenheim-bilbao.eus/en/about-the-museum/sustainability.

16 'ICA Miami Expands Sustainability Initiatives through Innovative Wind Energy Agreement with ENGIE', ENGIE press release, 5 July 2024, https://gems.engie.com/ica-miami-expands-sustainability-initiatives-through-innovative-wind-energy-agreement-with-engie.

17 Renewable Energy Certificates are known by various names worldwide, including Renewable Energy Guarantees of Origin (REGO) and Power Guarantee of Origin (GoO) in Europe. For more information see https://gems.engie.com/solution/energy-attribute-certificates/.

18 'Land Remediation', Forge Project, n.d., https://forgeproject.com/projects/land-remediation.

19 For a useful overview, see Jessica Kutz, 'Indigenous Land Trust Empowers Women to Reclaim and Restore Ancestral Land', *The 19th*, 22 November 2023, https://19thnews.org/2023/11/indigenous-land-trust-women-ancestry-rematriation.

20 This and subsequent quotes, interview with the author, July 2024.

21 Cliodhna Murphy, 'Sea Freight: Unlocking the Potential for International Art Transportation', 2 November 2023, https://www.hauserwirth.com/news/sea-freight-unlocking-the-potential-for-international-art-transportation/.

22 This and subsequent quotes, interview with the author, July 2024.

23 'Greener Galleries', Hauser & Wirth, n.d., https://www.hauserwirth.com/sustainability/.

24 'Introduction to GCC's New SCF Policy', Gallery Climate Coalition, 2024, https://galleryclimatecoalition.org/scfs/introduction-to-gccs-new-scf-policy/.

25 Annabel Keenan, 'Art World Organisations, Galleries and Artists Helped Fund Conservation of a Peruvian Cloud Forest', *The Art Newspaper*, 12 April 2022, https://www.theartnewspaper.com/2022/04/12/galleries-commit-conservation-peru-cloud-forest.

26 Email to the author, 14 August 2024.

27 Louisa Buck, 'Oceanic Kelp Forests Are Regrowing Thanks to Charity that Sells Art to Fund Carbon Capture Projects', *The Art Newspaper*, 13 January 2023, https://www.theartnewspaper.com/2023/01/13/oceanic-kelp-forests-are-regrowing-thanks-to-charity-that-sells-art-to-fund-carbon-capture-projects.

28 'Impact: Artists for ClientEarth', Gallery Climate Coalition, 23 June 2023, https://galleryclimatecoalition.org/news/64-impact-artists-for-clientearth/.

29 'Sustainability', Art Basel, n.d., https://www.artbasel.com/sustainability.

30 'Environmental Responsibility Statement', Frieze, n.d., https://www.frieze.

com/page/friezes-environmental-responsibility-statement.

31 'The Art Show 2023: Exhibitor Booth Report', Climate Impact Report, Artists Commit, April 2022, https://www.artistscommit.com/reports/adaa-art-show-2023.

32 Email to the author, 21 August 2024.

33 Email to the author, 20 August 2024.

34 This and subsequent quotes, interview with the author, June 2024.

35 This and subsequent quotes, interview with the author, July 2024.

36 This and subsequent quotes, interview with the author, July 2024.

37 Interview with the author, August 2024.

38 'Contribute to NEMO Mapping of Climate Action by European Museums', Network of European Museum Organisations, 30 November 2023, https://www.ne-mo.org/news-events/article/contribute-to-nemo-mapping-of-climate-action-by-european-museums.

39 Annabel Keenan, 'New International Climate Action Coalition Aims to Make the Art Industry Sustainable', *The Art Newspaper*, 8 July 2021, https://www.theartnewspaper.com/2021/07/08/new-international-climate-action-coalition-aims-to-make-the-art-industry-sustainable.

40 'Art Charter for Climate Action', United Nations Climate Change, n.d., https://unfccc.int/climate-action/sectoral-engagement/entertainment-and-culture-for-climate-action/art-charter-for-climate-action.

4: The Future of Climate Action in the Art World

1 Interview with the author, July 2024.

2 Jeff Goodell, 'Opinion: We Built Our World for a Climate that No Longer Exists', CNN, 12 July 2024, https://www.cnn.com/2024/07/12/opinions/climate-crisis-change-extreme-weather-infrastructure/index.html.

3 Chris Bastock, 'The Day the Thames Broke its Banks, and Flooded Tate Britain', Tate, n.d., https://www.tate.org.uk/visit/tate-britain/day-thames-broke-its-banks-and-flooded-tate-britain.

4 Karen McVeigh, 'Before the Flood: How much Longer Will the Thames Barrier Protect London', *The Guardian*, 30 June 2023, https://www.theguardian.com/environment/2023/jun/30/before-the-flood-how-much-longer-will-the-thames-barrier-protect-london.

5 Encompass HK, 'How Marginalised Groups Are Disproportionately

Affected by Climate Change', Earth.org, 9 November 2022, https://earth.org/marginalised-groups-are-disproportionately-affected-by-climate-change/.

6   Alique G. Berberian, David J.X. Gonzalez and Lara J. Cushing, 'Racial Disparities in Climate Change-Related Health Effects in the United States', Current Environmental Health Reports, 28 May 2022, https://www.ncbi.nlm.nih.gov/pmc/articles/PMC9363288/.

7   Annabel Keenan, 'Black Museums Face Greater Peril in the Climate Crisis', *The Art Newspaper*, 7 February 2024, https://www.theartnewspaper.com/2024/02/07/black-museums-face-greater-peril-in-the-climate-crisis.

8   'Climate Change Poses Major Threats to Black Museums', Association of African American Museums press release, December 2023.

9   Email to the author, 14 August 2024.

10 Interview with Heath Lowndes of GCC, August 2024.

Further Reading

Carson, Rachel, *Silent Spring* (HarperCollins Publishers, New York, 2002)

Ferry, Robert and Elizabeth Monoian, eds, *Land Art as Climate Action* (Hirmer Publishers, Munich, 2023)

Figueres, Christiana and Tom Rivett-Carnac, *The Future We Choose* (Penguin, New York, 2020)

Fowkes, Maja and Reuben Fowkes, *Art and Climate Change* (Thames & Hudson, New York, 2022)

Goodell, Jeff, *The Heat Will Kill You First* (Little, Brown & Company, New York, 2023)

Kastner, Jeffrey and Brian Wallis, eds, *Land and Environment Art* (Phaidon Press Limited, London, 1998)

Merriman, Nick, ed., *Museums and the Climate Crisis* (Routledge, Abingdon 2024)

Obrist, Hans Ulrich and Kostas Stasinopoulos, eds, *140 Artist Ideas for Planet Earth* (Penguin, London, 2022)

Solnit, Rebecca and Thelma Young Lutunatabua, eds, *Not Too Late: Changing the Climate Story from Despair to Possibility* (Haymarket Books, Chicago, 2023)

Thomas, Leah, *The Intersectional Environmentalist* (Hachette Book Group, New York, 2022)

Weintraub, Linda, *To Life! Eco Art in Pursuit of a Sustainable Future* (University of California Press, Berkeley and Los Angeles, 2012)

Welz, Adam, *The End of Eden* (Bloomsbury Publishing, New York, 2023)

Wiesenberger, Robert, ed., *Humane Ecology: Eight Positions* (Yale University Press, New Haven, CT, 2023)

Online Resources

Climate Action Database, https://www.galleriescommit.com/climate-action-database

Climate Impact Report, https://www.artistscommit.com/reports/how-to-climate-impact-report

Environmental Sustainability, https://www.aam-us.org/category/environmental-sustainability/

GCC Carbon Calculator, https://measure.galleryclimatecoalition.org

Ki Books, https://www.kiculture.org/ki-books/

STiCH Carbon Calculator, https://stich.culturalheritage.org/carbon-calculator/#browse

'Museums, Climate and Politics', Network of European Museum Organisations, https://www.ne-mo.org/fileadmin/Dateien/public/Publications/NEMO_Report_Museums_Climate_and_Politics_11.2023_01.pdf

'Rethinking the Sustainability of Logistics in the Global Art Scene', Artlogic, https://www.youtube.com/watch?v=MtuxClZxp2I&list=PLLijMOq34X6NX3wP69-psW3Lv_hb1wj0V&index=8

Index

Index

103